Today's Gift

D0710231

Today's Gift

Daily Meditations for Families

Illustrations by
David Spohn

First printing, June, 1985.

ISBN: 0-89486-302-9

Printed in the United States of America.

This book is dedicated to the memory of
J. D. Davis

INTRODUCTION

All that is human has been preserved and shaped across thousands of generations of families. Our ability to love in a certain way, our capacity for hate, our tendencies toward envy, generosity, cruelty, and self-sacrifice are the legacy of family.

This book is meant to help us celebrate and strengthen our families. The readings are intended to inspire discussion and self-expression, and to encourage us to learn from one another no matter what our age differences are. Most of us live in families of varied interests, each member going his or her own way most of each day. Here, then, with this book, is a chance to share a few minutes with one another — to renew our mutual trust and understanding and to take advantage of the wisdom we each have to offer.

By taking part in one another's development, we can assure ourselves the love and strength of those who know us best when we need it most. We also assure that positive change will be passed on through future generations. In this way, we lay our hands lovingly on the present, and the on future.

The editor

Acknowledgments

The following writers contributed their work to this book: Antiga, Paul Bjorklund, Cecil Carle, Liane Cordes, Paula Culp, Emilio DeGrazia, Karen Casey Elliott, Jeanne Englemann, Patricia Hoolihan, Bonnie-Jean Kimball, Joe Klaas, Roseann Lloyd, Peter McDonald, Beth Milligan, Ann Monson, Pat O'Donnell, and Cynthia Orange.

The design and illustrations were done by David Spohn.

January

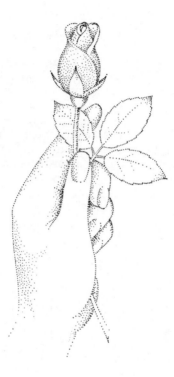

*The fragrance always stays in the hand
that gives the rose.*
                              —Hada Bejar

Nothing is more attractive than sharing with others. No trait will be admired as much as generosity. There is no surer way to gain the respect of friends and neighbors than to show by what we give that we care about others.

We can give many things besides money, shelter, clothing, or food to those in need. We can give the rich person love and understanding that money can't buy. We can be sympathetic with problems of those who are troubled, even though they appear wealthier than ourselves. We can share experience, strength, and hope with those who are ill or unhappy. We can even share our suffering with others who suffer, and hold up a light for them on the road to recovery.

What do I have to give today?

January 2

Happiness is like manna; it is to be gathered and enjoyed every day.
—*Tryon Edwards*

Life is like a winding path surrounded by flowers, butterflies, and delicious fruit, but many of us spend much of life looking for happiness around the next corner. We do not bend to enjoy the happiness which is ours for the taking just at our feet.

In our desire to reach the "pot of gold," the complete and lasting happiness we all want to fill our lives, we ignore anything which doesn't seem worthy of such a large ambition, or which can't give us the whole thing all at once.

Happiness is all around us, but it often comes in small grains. When we gather it grain by grain, we soon have a basketful.

What small pieces of my happiness surround me right now?

Time is a dressmaker specializing in alterations.

—*Faith Baldwin*

Change surrounds us. It lies within us, too. The trees in the yard have changed. They've grown taller. Their leaves die and scatter on the ground in the fall. We don't resemble our baby pictures much any more, either. Like trees, we've grown up. As babies, we couldn't walk. But we learned to run, ride bikes, go out alone to movies and parties.

Some changes we don't notice while they're going on. The snow melts; the birds fly south; our hair grows a little every day. Other changes startle us. A best friend moves away. Perhaps a favorite grandparent dies. These changes we wish hadn't happened, and we have to remember that change is as natural as breathing. We can't keep it from happening, but we can trust that change never means to harm us. It's a sign we're growing up.

What changes may occur today?

January 4

A tip-off to an abusive family system is a situation in which nobody ever apologizes.

—Karen Shaud

When we get a tip-off, we can open the door to a whole new way of looking at the world. The tip-off about apologies can help us learn to have a healthier family. It is hard to apologize, but, with practice, it will get easier.

We are learning we can make mistakes, admit them, and other people will accept our apologies. In the same way, we are learning we can accept others' apologies. Apologies are sometimes hard to make. It helps to keep in mind that we make them as much for ourselves, and our own growth, as for the person we apologize to. We are not worthless just because we make mistakes, but we increase our value to ourselves and others by being able to recognize them and apologize.

Is there an apology I need to make today?

*. . .and, when the time comes to let it
go,. . .let it go.*

—*Mary Oliver*

If we all let go of one thing we like, and take
instead each other's hand; if we all let go of three
minutes each day, and find instead a few perfect
words for someone in the house; if we all withhold
our judgments for one hour, and reveal during that
time one of our own small secret sins; if we all skip
the same meal each week, and spend the time together in the park; would we have less or more
than what we started with?

It is one of the great and pleasing mysteries of
life that we gain by giving things up. Instead of
grabbing things, or demanding from others if we
give something up, that leaves a space for something new to enter our lives.

Can I get more out of life by expecting less today?

January 6

We, too, the children of the earth, have our moon phases all through any year; the darkness, the delivery from darkness, the waxing and waning.
                    —*Faith Baldwin*

Let us think, for a moment, about the changes of the moon. In the beginning of its cycle, it is just a sliver in the darkness. Each night it grows larger until it reaches its full size. When the moon is full and rising, its orange glow fills the sky. All night its gentle light brightens everything it touches.

But this fullness is only part of the life of the moon. For a while it grows smaller, then turns its dark side toward us before reappearing as a sliver and growing again to fullness.

We are children of the earth, and we have our different moods and phases, too. There will be periods of darkness when we try to find our way by the light of the stars. Again and again we will grow to our full size, only to fade and grow again in a new way.

How does God light my way, even in dark times?

*To affect the quality of the day — that
is the highest of the arts.*
        —*Henry David Thoreau*

We are the sculptors of our day. We can mold it
creatively into a wonderful masterpiece. We control the amount of moisture we mix into our clay.
We pound it, shape it, stroke it, love it. Others can
offer suggestions and we gain new perspectives
from their advice, but it is finally our own creation. Our knife may occasionally slip, or our mixture of earth may be too dry. Any great artist suf-
fers temporary setbacks. Besides, imperfections in
art often make it all the more interesting.

How creative can I be in my life today?

January 8

> *Deep in their roots all flowers keep the light.*
> —*Theodore Roethke*

All flowers begin with the potential to grow and blossom. Yet in winter, perennial flowers are buried under the snow. Inside the dark earth, they are patiently waiting for their time to bloom. For the flowers, faith is believing that spring will return. It is carrying the light of summer deep in their roots — so that even in times of cold and dark, there is hope that they will bloom again.

When spring does return, they shoot out of the ground and burst into blossom. In times of light, they drink it deep into their roots — deep enough to sustain them through the next season of darkness.

We can do the same, keeping the memory of good times deep within us, so that when we're feeling low, it will keep our faith in the happy future strong.

What helps sustain my faith today?

*Life gives us so much time to collect
bizarre thoughts and feelings.*
        —Claire Weekes

As we go through life, we run into all kinds of negative messages: teasing on the school bus, insulting nicknames, and other put-downs.

Pretty soon we may discover that some of these messages stick in our minds, repeating themselves over and over like broken records. These messages can make us feel bad about ourselves. But when we hear one of these tapes playing inside us, we have the power to push the STOP button. Then we can record a new message. We can even say it out loud, so that our voice settles emphatically into our thoughts.

We can't make others stop saying these things, but we can stop listening to them. They only have power over us when we give it to them. We have the ability and freedom to let negative thoughts float by us, like water going downstream.

What positive message can I send to myself?

January 10

> *You feel the way you do right now because of the thoughts you are thinking at this moment.*
>
> —*David D. Burns*

Good thoughts are like bright colors in a painting. Negative thoughts are dark and dreary and drab. Each day we paint pictures of our own lives with our thoughts. If we step back and look at the canvas, we will see whether the picture is alive with bright colors or dreary and lifeless like a dark cloud.

Our thoughts have the power to bring joy or sadness our way, depending on what we expect or look for in our surroundings.

The choice of how we want our lives to be is ours. Since we paint a new picture each day, we are always free to change things when they don't please us. What better time than the present?

Is there something in my life I'd like to change today?

It does make a difference what you call things.
        —*Kate Douglas Wiggin*

Most of us think of dandelions as weeds. We buy special tools and poisons when they crop up and complain about them as surely as we welcome the spring that brings them.

Yet is there anything more lovely than a sea of yellow dandelions by the side of the road in June? Or as remarkable in transformation as the filaments of the mature dandelion blowing on the wind?

Sometimes we let someone else define for us what are weeds and what are flowers. We don't have to. Much of the beauty of the world is that we ourselves decide what is beautiful according to our own feelings. How lucky we are that, when we choose to, we can open our eyes and see!

Can I see the beauty in those around me right now?

January 12

> *I held a moment in my hand, brilliant
> as a star, fragile as a flower, a shiny
> sliver out of one hour. I dropped it
> carelessly. O God! I knew not I held an
> opportunity.*
>
> —Hazel Lee

Once, a famous artist was hired to put the stained glass windows into a great cathedral. His eager young apprentice pleaded for the chance to design just one small window. The master artist feared an experiment on even a small window would prove costly, but the persistent young apprentice kept up his pleas. Finally, the master agreed that he could try his hand on one small window if he furnished his own materials and worked on his own time.

The enterprising apprentice began gathering bits of glass his master had discarded, and set to work. When the cathedral doors were open, people stood in groups before the small window, praising its delicate excellence.

Our lives are like this. If we take the time to gather together the moments and opportunities we too often discard and waste, we find we can weave them into something beautiful.

What can I make of moments I usually waste today?

Home is the place where, when you have to go there, they have to take you in.

—*Robert Frost*

Our home is a place of roots, a place where we can always turn in time of need. Some of us may have had the experience of being away from home and not been able to make it on our own. We know what a relief it was to at last reach out and call our family, who we knew would take us in.

We became people in our homes, we learned to eat and walk and talk there. We feel comfortable there, safe from the pressures of the outside world. It is up to us to keep it safe and healthy by growing in love and generosity there.

Home is a place to really give of ourselves and put our best into making it happy and secure. It will affect our futures more than almost anything else in our lives. It deserves our prayers of blessing. It is our foundation, the source of our first feelings for others. May we treasure our home and the people who make up our family.

What small thing can I do right now to make home a better place?

January 14

The universe is made up of stories, not atoms.

—*Muriel Rukeyser*

There was once a storyteller who told many people of her life. They listened and heard their own stories in hers. Hearing her story, they didn't feel so lonely any more. Hearing about someone else who had lost things and people she loved, who had felt lonely, scared, and unsure of herself, let them feel less crazy when similar things happened to them.

Because of the healing they felt through hearing someone else's story, some of the listeners decided to become storytellers themselves. As they recounted their stories, they found that letting out secrets which had bothered them for years freed them to feel good about who they were and who they had always wanted to be.

What secrets can I share today?

*Always remember that no matter what
the problem may be, there is an infinity
of solutions.*
—*Marion Weinstein*

A girl named Iris was tormented by the boys at school. Whenever she walked by they would make rude noises. Sometimes, when no one was looking, they would block her way and not let her go home. She was too inexperienced at taking care of herself to realize that believing she couldn't do anything made it true. Feeling helpless kept her from thinking about what she might do.

One day she got so scared that she told her best friend what was happening. Together they began to think of all sorts of things she could do. Knowing she could do something took away the helpless feeling, and the boys noticed and stopped teasing her. It wasn't fun for them anymore.

We often feel helpless in situations that seem too much for us to handle. In fact, help is always available — through friends and family, and through God, who helps us see how we can help ourselves. All we have to do is stop being distracted by that helpless feeling and ask for what we need.

Can I see the many solutions to my problems today?

January 16

When you do something you are proud of, dwell on it a little, praise yourself for it.

—Mildred Newman

Each one of us is very good at something. Maybe it's baseball or tennis where we display talent. Maybe we're good in math or at giving reports. A few people are talented at being good listeners or helpful friends. To recognize our own talents we may need help from others. It's always so much easier to see our faults, or the ways we don't meet our own expectations.

But the fact is we are all skilled in many areas of our lives. To accept praise, better yet, to quietly give it to ourselves, is a sign of healthy growth.

What things have I done well lately?

*Man cannot remake himself without
suffering. For he is both the marble and
the sculptor.*
— *Alexis Carrell*

A sculptor begins with an unformed piece of
marble. He must be able to envision what he wants
to create. Then, armed with tools and courage, he
begins to chink away at the marble he does not
need. Every day he examines how it looks and
what he wants it to become.

Every one of us who is trying to be a better
person is like the sculptor. We envision who we
want to be and what kind of qualities we believe
in. Some of these qualities might be kindness,
good self-esteem, the ability to love and feel loved.
If we are honest, we must also look with the artist's eye at our faults. We might see some jealousy
and resentment, or feelings of superiority. Our
faults, human as they are, are like unwanted marble that keeps our most loving selves from taking
shape. Carving away at our faults is hard work,
and sometimes even hurts. Yet we do not do this
work alone — we can only do it with the help of
our God.

What can I chisel away today?

January 18

> *The stream that was locked up for the
> winter now ripples and gurgles along its
> way.*
>
> —*John F. Gardner*

Winter presents us with a frozen world, silent,
sometimes forbidding. It seems like such a harsh
time, forcing us indoors, letting us out only when
we're wrapped in extra woolens, extra boots, extra
hats and mittens. But beneath the snow's blanket,
the earth is resting. Just as we sleep at night, the
earth naps, nurturing its roots and bulbs, replen-
ishing its moisture and minerals, refreshing itself.
Spring is the earth's first stirring; it opens one eye,
then another, wiggles a toe, stretches, yawns. The
earth rises, shaking leaves off, brushing twigs
away. It sends new shoots up to welcome the day.

We, too, are part of nature, and as such we
experience our own seasons. Sometimes we are
happy, full of energy, always able to handle obstacles. When we are down; when things seem to be
too much for us to handle, we must remember that
it is natural and proper to feel that way, and that
soon, without our even trying, a new season will
lift our hearts.

When I feel low, what can I do best?

*A journey of a thousand miles must
begin with a single step.*
—*Chinese Proverb*

Even the strongest, most loving families always
have room for growth. There is no such thing as a
"perfect" family. If our family is far from perfect,
that's okay. It only matters that we are working at
getting better. Often, runners who need to practice
will say they can remember many days when they
just did not feel like running. However, once they
started, they felt more energy and were easily able
to run the distance they had set for that day.

Whatever we need to do, we can do in small
acts — a chore done without being asked, a helping hand with the dishes, a soft word, a surprise
gift for no reason. These are small things, easily
done. Love is made of small things, what is large is
the love with which they are accompanied.

When we begin to work on our relationship
with our family, we will feel the new energy, and
quickly we will find ourselves making progress.

*What is the first thing I can do today to improve
my relationship with my family?*

January 20

The power of a man's virtue should not be measured by his special efforts, but by his ordinary doing.

—Blaise Pascal

The airplane kit is on the table in front of us. We have the glue, the little wooden pieces, and the instructions. We work for hours putting together each piece, step by step. A dab of glue here, a clamp there, maybe some rubber bands to hold the bigger pieces together. We work slowly, allowing the glue to set overnight, even though we want to see it fly right now.

We follow each step in order, even though we think we know how to do it on our own. Patience is the most important asset we bring to this activity — the willingness to allow each step its own time and proper place.

After we've done all the careful work and waited till the glue is firm, we take it out for a trial flight. It soars! So do we, when we allow ourselves time to learn each step of the way.

What part of my future am I assembling today?

*If you realize you aren't so wise today
as you thought you were yesterday,
you're wiser today.*

—Olin Miller

Smug was a kitten who thought she knew everything. She knew how to clean herself with her sandpaper tongue; how to sleep, eat, and keep warm, and how to sharpen her tiny claws.

One day, her mother wanted to teach Smug to climb trees. I don't need to learn this, thought Smug, I already know everything I need to know.

Without much interest, Smug watched her mother climb a tall tree and come down again. When it came to Smug's turn, she said, "I'll stay on the ground where it's safe." Just then, a large black dog came trotting around the corner.

Aren't we often like Smug, certain we know all we need to know, or that we really don't need to know something another is trying to teach us? When we rid ourselves of the pride that keeps us from learning these things, we'll feel a little safer if any big black dogs come around the corner. And we will have grown smarter by recognizing our need to know more.

Am I smart enough to admit my need to learn more today?

January 22

Animals are such agreeable friends they ask no questions, they pass no criticisms.

—George Eliot

A pet is often liked by everyone and seems to have no enemies. Why is this? Pets are friendly and interested in others. They seem to get joy out of just being with us. They do not have a critical attitude. When mistreated or neglected for a while, they are quick to forgive, and quickly seek once again to be by our side.

Each of us is a valuable part of the family. When we treasure one another, and don't waste our time finding each other's faults, we will begin to have less faults. When we accept our loved ones as they are, and enjoy sharing our lives with them, our lives become more enjoyable, and our family love grows because we are each more loveable.

What can I accept in others today?

Little girl, little girl, where have you been?

—*Mother Goose*

She's been everywhere and nowhere in and around the house. She's been in her room crying with her doll, on the grass kicking her ball, on the floor big-eyed and blank in front of the TV. Her things are everywhere in the way, as if left there to block the path. She learns to be happiest alone in her room. There she can gather roses to give to the Queen and receive in return a diamond as big as a shoe. There she can wait for some prince, or dream of crossing the street without looking back.

We are all the same way, even as adults. We live with our dreams and fantasies, and our secret lives thrive in privacy.

All around us, our loved ones live out their private lives often unnoticed by us until we enter them. When we honor others' unspoken needs, when we allow others their privacy without being asked, or when we appreciate something they've done, we share the joy of living together in natural harmony.

How invisible are those in our presence every day?

January 24

Only with winter-patience
can we bring
The deep desired, long-awaited
spring.
— *Anne Morrow Lindbergh*

Family life requires patience. We probably realized that a long time ago. The Greek origin of the word *patience* is *pathos,* which means "suffering." In our lives together, we often suffer. Life is full of bumps and scrapes, both physical and emotional. In our search for greater family unity and harmony we need to realize that we will not be able to escape all suffering. This is why we need patience. It is a form of love.

When we suffer the bumps and scrapes and still have faith something good will come of it, we are living out our love. From this winter-patience we will surely find a reward.

How have I practiced my patience already today?

Muddy water, let stand, becomes clear.
—Lao-tzu

A group of friends went swimming one day and one of them lost a quarter in the bottom of the lake. Everyone started diving from different directions to find it until there was so much mud and sand stirred up that no one could see anything. Finally, they decided to clear the water. They waited silently on the edge of the shore for the mud from all their activity to settle. When it finally cleared, one person dove in slowly and picked up the quarter.

When we are confused about something in our lives, we will often hear answers and advice from all directions. Our friends will tell us one thing and our families another, until we feel pretty well mixed up. If we look away from our problem and let patience and time do their work, the mud inside us will settle and clear. Our answer will become visible, like the glimmer of silver in the water.

Am I overlooking the simple solution?

January 26

*Nothing is more difficult than compet-
ing with a myth.*

—Francoise Giroud

Sometimes we think we need to try and be
something we're not. Maybe we feel pressure from
friends to behave or dress like someone else. All we
need to do is remember when we were younger
and dressed in our parents' clothes and shoes. We
pretended to be grownups and it was fun for a
while. Then the huge shoes on our feet grew
clumsy and uncomfortable and the mountain of
rolled-up sleeves kept falling down and getting in
the way. Soon we grew tired of the game and
stopped pretending.

Today, when we start feeling the pressure to be
someone else, let's remember how hard it is to play
a role that doesn't fit us.

What can I do today that is most like me?

*When men are rightfully occupied,
then their amusement grows out of
their work as the color petals out of a
fruitful garden.*

—*John Ruskin*

What do we need most in order to be happy?
Certainly we all need to be loved. Yet we need even
more than that. The spirit also wishes to be
needed. When we are needed, no matter what age
we are, we serve a purpose for others. When we
are needed, we will be loved as well as respected,
imitated, and rewarded with gratitude.

Our needs are not great empty pits to be filled
any way we can. They are the couplings by which
we connect to those we love. Our needs tell us also
what others want, and how to enrich their lives —
which also enriches ours.

How do we become needed? We have only to
look at our own needs and give what we need to
others — love, respect, kindness, generosity.
When we realize we are needed, we realize we also
need others.

*What do I need that I can give to another person
today?*

January 28

It is such a secret place, the land of tears.
　　　　　—Antoine de St. Exupery

Where do tears come from? Perhaps each of us has a private well where the tears rise from. Each of us has our own landscape of events that have hurt us or given us joy. And so we have our own private responses to the world around us. Something may hurt one of us that would not hurt another.

Like the oceans and rivers, sometimes our well of tears is flowing. We do not always understand all the forces affecting the oceans, or our well of tears.

The kind of bucket that draws water from a well is solid and durable and it lowers itself deep enough to find water. Good friends and family members are like that. It is comforting to share our private well with such people.

Who will I invite to drink from my well today?

Think in terms of depletion, not depression. . . . You can understand how a body can replenish itself, whereas it may be difficult to understand the way out of depression.

—Claire Weekes

Despair and depression may come over us suddenly, for no reason we can figure out. But if we stop and reflect, we may realize we are reacting to too much of something — too much work, too much excitement, too much fun. We may be having a letdown after holidays, after completing a project, or at the end of a school year.

When we feel a letdown coming on, we must give ourselves time. We need to take some time off and do nothing, plan nothing. Then we can ask God to help us let go of the negative feelings that come along with a letdown.

We can plan a small gift for ourselves — a walk by the lake, for instance. In our excitement with a rush of events, we often forget that we, like the infants we once were, need to take a rest and reenergize.

Do I need to do something just for myself today?

Everyone has his own fingerprints. The white light streams down to be broken up by those human prisms into all the colors of the rainbow. Take your own color in the pattern and be just that.
　　　　　　　　　　—*Charles R. Brown*

We are often amazed at how different members of the same family seem to be. Contrasts are often great: one child might be loud and funny, one might be timid and quiet, and yet neither seems to take after the parents.

A family is like a vegetable garden. The vegetables respond to outside influences. The one exposed to more sunlight will grow differently than the one growing in a damp, shady place. Vegetables growing in crowded areas of the garden may not be as developed as those around them, but they might be tastier.

Although we may have common roots, outside experiences and friends mold us, too, making each of us unique. We sometimes lose ourselves by comparisons and feel like we don't belong, but the variety of our family garden is what makes the world so interesting!

How can I honor another person's uniqueness today?

Thou shalt not should *thyself.*
—*Anonymous*

When someone tells us we *should* do something, do we want to do it, or do we feel mad that someone else is telling us what we want to do? Sometimes we forget that these messages are not our own, but are the desires of others. It's important to listen to what we tell ourselves, to be aware of which messages we're giving ourselves and which come from others.

We can make a list of all our *shoulds* and identify where they came from: parent, boss, friend, self. Then we can decide which *shoulds* are *want tos,* and throw out the rest. Doing what we want to is very different from doing what we should, and we can usually do a better job of it.

Have I freed myself of shoulds today?

February

It's not enough to talk to plants; you also have to listen.
—*David Bergman*

Plants grow best when we pay attention to them. That means watering, touching them, putting them in places where they will receive good light. They need people around them, to notice if they are drooping at the edges or looking particularly happy in the sunlight. The more attention a plant receives, the better it will grow.

We need to be noticed in the same way. If we notice a family member or friend is drooping, perhaps we can pay some special attention to them. All of us need someone to care about how we are and to truly listen to us. We can share and double someone's happiness by noticing and talking about it also. We help the people around us to grow by listening to their droopy edges as well as their bright days. People need this as much as plants need light and water.

How can I help someone grow today?

February 2

Fear is the absence of faith.
—*Paul Tillich*

We all experience fear. Sometimes we fear small things that only seem large at the time, like a test in school, or meeting a new boss, or going to the dentist. Sometimes we fear big things like serious illness or death, or that someone we love will come to harm. Fear is healthy, and we all feel it. It keeps us from doing foolish things sometimes, but too much fear can also keep us from doing what we need for our growth.

If we have faith in God and in ourselves, we can turn and face whatever frightens us, believing we can, with help, do what seems impossible. And we will, and the fear will vanish. The important first step in dealing with fear is to take action — either by tackling what we fear ourselves, or by asking for help. Each time we face our fear, we gain strength, courage, and confidence in the doing.

What am I most afraid of?

In a hole in the ground there lived a hobbit. Not a nasty, dirty, wet hole . . . nor yet a dry, bare, sandy hole with nothing in it . . . it was a hobbithole, and that means comfort.
—*J. R. R. Tolkien*

Home is a place of comfort. When we go away and have to adjust to a different bed and someone else's cooking, we quickly discover how comfortable our own home is. Comfort in a home is more than just a familiar bed and favorite food, it is something we can give to each other. We can make home a place where we can relax and be ourselves without fear of rejection.

Each of us needs a special little place where we can come and seek refuge from the world, our own little "fort." Children are often busy making "forts," but all of us in the family need to work at making the place where we live together a fort where we can all gather for rest.

What can I add to our comfort today?

February 4

The shy man usually finds that he has been shy without cause, and that, in practice, no one takes the slightest notice of him.

—*Robert Lynd*

We sometimes feel self-conscious in front of others. It may be that we've just gotten braces or a new haircut and we're afraid everyone will stare at us. We stop smiling and talk with our heads bowed. Many people have worn braces and many more will. We need not be ashamed just because we feel different. By beginning to smile again we will see how many people really didn't notice our braces, or our haircuts, or anything but what they see inside us.

All we need to do is lift our heads and smile. We will be amazed to find how little even our best friends notice about the externals, the things that don't really matter. Who we are is far more noticeable and far more important than what we look like. A smile at shy times helps us accept ourselves as others do.

What makes me shy?

Let there be spaces in your together-ness.
　　　　　　　　—*Kahlil Gibran*

Sometimes it is just as important to know when to leave others alone as it is to know when to talk with them. We all need to be alone at times — to think, to work out a problem, or just to be quiet with ourselves. This is especially true in families, where we're often surrounded by others. If we tune in to our other family members, we can develop sensors that will let us know when they need some time alone. Part of good communication is knowing when *not* to talk too.

Can I be sensitive to my family's needs for privacy today?

February 6

> *Pride works from within; it is the direct appreciation of oneself.*
> —Arthur Schopenhauer

Pride, like all emotions, has two faces, one healthy and one sick. It is our challenge to use the healthy side well. Sick pride fills us with ourselves, looks down on others, and has no room for generosity. Healthy pride is heavy with humility. If we can feel joyful when we succeed, and tell others about it honestly, we are not being boastful.

Sick pride often keeps us from doing things because we are too proud to ask for help when we need it, or too proud to risk failure, or to do anything that might not turn out perfect.

Healthy pride about our greatest victories always comes with the awareness that we did not do it all by ourselves. We had the aid, advice, and encouragement of loved ones. In all things that really count, we never walk alone. Even those who claim pride is not a virtue admit that it is parent of many virtues.

What makes me proud of myself today?

*It is the weak who are cruel. Gentleness
can only be expected from the strong.*
— Leo Rosten

When we think of strength, do we think of
someone who shows no emotion and intimidates
others with physical power? True strength is freedom to show all kinds of feelings. Strong people
aren't afraid of being vulnerable. A person who
feels insecure may not feel free to show any kind of
softness or be able to share gentle feelings. If we
have true inner strength, we are not afraid to show
what is a part of us, gentle feelings included.

It is wonderful to see a well-conditioned athlete
cry tears of joy after a victory. In such an example
we can see physical and emotional strength. In our
lives together, we will be stronger if we do not try
to hide our feelings out of fear. As our feelings
flow, we will increase our self-understanding and
build our true strength.

*Am I strong enough to show how I really feel to-
day?*

February 8

When I look back on all these worries I remember the story of the old man who said on his deathbed that he had had a lot of trouble in his life, most of which never happened.

—Winston Churchill

A rolled-up ball of yarn does not take up much space — it sits, ready to be used when needed. It gets unrolled a little bit at a time — just as much as is needed and no more. But a ball of yarn that gets unravelled can be strewn across an entire room. It becomes a jumbled mass, entangled and confusing.

When we live our lives a day at a time, we are like that rolled-up ball of yarn. Our thoughts, feelings, and skills are ready to be used as they are needed. But when we worry, our spirit becomes a jumbled mass of yarn. We get ahead of and behind ourselves — our thoughts are scattered and often our feelings are confused. Worry adds clutter and confusion to life.

What is most helpful is to put the worry away — to roll up the ball of yarn and bring ourselves into the present moment. In this way, we stand ready for each new stitch — and we will never be given more than we are able to handle.

Do I have worries which are cluttering my life today?

Leave yourself alone.
                    —*Jenny Janacek*

Three women were talking. One blamed herself for an unkind remark someone had made to her. Another blamed herself for not getting work done. The other compared her looks to those of the movie stars and thought she was ugly.

The women each noticed how the other two had put themselves down without being aware of it, and they began to laugh. Then they vowed to be as kind to themselves as they were to each other. Each time they caught themselves being mean to themselves, they imagined they were their own best friend, and were as understanding to themselves as they were to one another.

When we are kind to ourselves, only then can we be truly kind to others, and make ourselves a gift to those around us.

How have I been kind to myself lately?

February 10

*A bird does not sing because he has an
answer. He sings because he has a song.*
—Joan Walsh Anglund

Each of us has a song to sing, just like birds do.
Part of knowing who we are is appreciating our
own songs. Are our songs gentle like the robin's, or
are we brilliant leaders like the bluejay? Are we
easy to be around like the sparrow, or do we radi-
ate joy and laughter like the loon?

Each of these birds has something special to offer. So do we, with our own unique personalities
and talents. What a waste it would be if the loon
never dashed across the lake because he wanted to
be a robin instead. It is important to learn who we
are and to believe we are special in our own way.
We give joy to the world around us when we sing
our own songs.

Have I listened to my own song lately?

*Life deals more rigorously with some
than others.*
— *Lewis F. Presnall*

How often we think about a friend, He sure is
lucky! And probably just as often we say to ourselves, Why did that happen to me? It's not fair!
The truth is, life isn't always fair. We don't all get
the same experiences, the same lessons. But we
each learn what we need to learn in order to fulfill
our destiny.

We have to learn to trust. Maybe a bike gets
stolen or a friend moves away. It's not easy to accept such things as these, but we must all learn to
understand and accept losses in our lives.

Perhaps we fail a test. The lesson we learn from
this may be to study harder or to consider a different course of study in school. There are always
reasons for why things happen, but we don't have
to know them.

Can I trust in the lessons of my failures today?

February 12

*Oh, a trouble's a ton, or a trouble's
    an ounce,
Or a trouble is what you
    make it,
And it isn't the fact that you're hurt
    that counts,
But only how you take it.*
                    —Edmund Vance Cooke

Once, a woman decided to throw a problem-exchange party. As guests arrived, they shed all their personal problems and tossed them onto a pile with everyone else's. After all had discussed their own problem for others to hear, the party ended with guests selecting from the problem pile those they wished to carry away. Each person left with the same troubles he or she had brought to the party.

We who worry a great deal about our problems are always sure no one else has troubles as bad as ours. Too often, we complain, "If you had my problems, you'd really hurt." Our problems are tailored to us, and geared to help us learn by solving them. No one else's would be quite right.

When we cope with problems, rather than wailing about them, we discover that our own are minor irritations compared to those we see in others.

What problems am I lucky to have?

"Shall I give you a kiss?" Peter asked,
and jerking an acorn button off his
coat, solemnly presented it to her.
                              —James Barrie

If kisses can be made of acorn buttons, they can
be made of any good thing. Think of kisses made
of candy. Therefore, there must be a thousand and
one ways to give a kiss. We can give one made of
wild flowers picked in the ditch, the melody in a
music box, the few true words in a note, or the
picture we ourselves draw to give to the one we
love. Think of how we can hide them here and
there under pillows, in corners, in pockets where
they're sure to be seen and felt. Think of how
hearts kiss when we hug or hold hands, how sleeping beauties suddenly wake up.

Does it matter that we try new ways to show our
same old love?

February 14

*Love cures people — both the ones who
give it and the ones who receive it.*
                                    —Karl Menninger

Receiving a loving hug from a parent, or perhaps a smile from a friend, or even a stranger,
gives us a special feeling inside. We know we are
important to others when they show us their love
through attention. And we sometimes forget that
we matter to others. Family members and friends
feel good in the same way when we show them our
love. Everyone needs to be loved.

How can we show our love? Must it be through
a hug? Doing a favor for someone is loving. Helping around the house or the yard is loving, particularly when we've volunteered our help. Giving an
unexpected gift to a friend is a way of showing
love. Showing someone we care, even when they
are angry, is perhaps the nicest of all expressions of
love.

What new way can I show someone I care today?

It is always a mistake not to close one's eyes, whether to forgive or to look better into oneself.
—*Maurice Maeterlinck*

It is easy to look outward and find faults with the world and people around us. We criticize family members or complain about our friends. Always, we notice disease in the trees around us.

But if we take time to be quiet, to sit alone in a tree or by a lake, we become more aware of how connected we are to the life around us. We are part of the beauty and the imperfection. When we notice our own tree is not perfect, it becomes easier to forgive the blights of those around us. It is also important to forgive ourselves our faults. Though all the trees are beautiful, they each have their scars. Being human means we are, like all humanity, both beautiful and imperfect.

Will I see through the flaws to another's beauty today?

February 16

> *Shame-filled people feel that something is wrong at their very core. It is a sense of being bad. . . .*
>
> —Susan Kwiecien

Nobody is rotten to the core. Whenever we start to believe we are bad all the way through, we can picture good things we have done, days when someone else was happy to be with us, and see for ourselves that we have many good points which outweigh the bad.

If we have done something wrong, we must apologize and make amends. Making a mistake is not the same as being worthless. Mistakes are a natural part of living, not something to be ashamed of. Our freedom to make mistakes is one of our greatest assets, for this is the way we learn humility, persistence, courage to take risks, and better ways of doing things. All of us are valuable and lovable. How could we be otherwise? Since mistakes are natural aspects of growth, we can salute them in ourselves and others as signs of life, and celebrate our ability to learn and to forgive.

What mistakes have helped me grow?

*There is glory
In a great mistake.*
              —*Nathalia Crane*

Once there was a big girl who liked to play with little kids and their toys. One day she rode one of their small bikes and her foot slipped off the little pedal and her leg got caught and dragged along the sidewalk.

She went home, limping and howling. Her mother put ice on the terrible scrape. The next day, the girl's mother told her she was too big for the little kids' toys. The girl looked up defiantly and said, "I can TOO ride that baby bike!"

The girl's mother didn't say anything else. She knew people must be free to make mistakes. We cannot protect another person from the experiences of the world. It would be harmful to both of us to try.

What mistakes have I made more than once before I learned my lesson?

February 18

> *United souls are not satisfied with embraces, but desire to be truly each other. . . .*
>
> —Sir Thomas Browne

If hugs could melt, if kisses were made of nothing but pure air, if talkers always agreed, and if hearts all beat to the same drum, would we desire any longer to be truly each other? No two leaves on a tree turn the same way in the wind; no two fish in a school tread the same water; and no two people can live the same life. Therefore, when we hug let's leave some space; when we kiss let's allow each other to breathe; when we talk let's permit each other to disagree; when we love let's honor each other's rhythm and way.

Is it our similarities or differences that make us want to know each other better?

I have often thought morality may perhaps consist solely in the courage of making a choice.
—Leon Blum

Sometimes, trying to do the right thing isn't easy because it isn't what we want to do. For instance, we may want to sneak a cookie to take to bed with us, or we may want to stay out late. But is that the right thing to do?

One way to tell is to think how we'll feel after we've done it. Will we be happy, or will we feel guilty because we know in our hearts it is wrong? On the other hand, how would we feel if we resisted the temptation? Perhaps we'd feel great because we'd know in our hearts we'd done the right thing. And don't we deserve to feel good about ourselves? Of course we do!

How wonderful it is that our feelings can help us do the right thing when we're in doubt.

Will I have the courage to follow my true feelings today?

February 20

Say what you like: say I'm ill,
Say I broke my leg on the stairs,
Say we've had a fire.

—T. S. Eliot

Think of the trouble of excuses and lies. They force us to make ourselves sick, live with a whole broken leg, start some sort of slow burn. When we tell someone we're not at home, we have to hide in that place. When we invent a long line of lies, we have to memorize each one. It's easiest just to come clean, use plain and simple words, and speak true. When accusers spear us with their stares, we can disarm them by looking them right in the eye.

Not only do lies deceive others, they keep us hidden from ourselves, and make our real reasons for the choices we've made seem unworthy, if we feel we can't express them. Better that we be truthful, even if a little pain results. Truth keeps communication lines open. Then, when someone really wants to know what's on our minds, we can simply open our hearts.

Is anything too terrible to tell to a friend?

We cannot do all things.

—*Virgil*

We are each limited in terms of time and energy. If we try to do too much, we do everything half-rate. How much better it is to clearly sort out what is really important to us, and then give ourselves to those things or people wholeheartedly.

Famous writers have written about the difficulty of having more than one or two really good friends. That number seems so unimpressive if we equate popularity with the number of friends we have. If we want quality, we must accept our limitations. In this way we avoid wasting energy on unimportant tasks, on friends who aren't true or close, on goals which aren't what we really want. We can only commit ourselves wholeheartedly to a limited number of tasks and a limited number of people.

Who are my truly good friends?

February 22

*In spite of everything I still believe that
people are really good at heart.*
                                    —Anne Frank

In the face of being hunted for extermination,
Anne Frank could write this from her hiding place
in an attic. Was she naive? No. She deeply believed in the goodness of creation and the goodness of all creatures, including those who perse-
cuted and murdered her people.

Somehow, young as she was, Anne Frank knew
a truth we sometimes lose: that it is not what people do that makes them good or evil. It is who they
are. And for Anne Frank, all people are made in
the image of God — and therefore, deep down at
their core, must be good. She was able to see
through the brutality and hatred to that true creation of God.

We are left in awe at such faith and love. But we
can draw from it, too, and when our brother or
sister or parent or child does something to hurt us,
we can remember Anne Frank's ability to see what
is good. We can look beneath the hurtful actions
and forgive.

Can I forgive someone who has hurt me today?

A person's best ally is someone who takes care of herself.
                                    —Susan Clarke

Once there was a little girl who was learning to walk. The trouble was, her mother wouldn't let her fall down. Every time she was about to fall, her mother would rush over and catch her.

It was hard to learn how to walk if she couldn't fall down, but the girl was too little to be able to tell her mother. Her mother thought she was taking care of her when in fact she was keeping her from learning to take care of herself. Letting her fall would have shown trust in the child, trust that she could get up. It would have taught her that she wasn't so fragile that she couldn't recover if she hurt herself.

We are all like this mother once in a while, protecting one another from important lessons in life. This doesn't mean we have to let someone get seriously hurt, but that we allow each other the freedom to learn and grow in individual ways.

What will I be able to learn from my little stumbles today?

February 24

*Thoughts — just mere thoughts — are
as powerful as electric batteries — as
good for one as sunlight is, or as bad
for one as poison.*
—Frances Hodgson Burnett

The truck was in mud to its axles. Three lumber-jacks sat in stony silence in the cab. There they were, stuck in the woods on their way to the cutting site. The first man slammed the steering wheel, cursed, and stormed out of the truck. The second thought the early morning woods inviting, and said he'd just crawl under a pine to nap until someone came along to pull them out. The third man, left alone, grabbed an axe and a saw and set about cutting wood to slide under the wheels. Within an hour he managed to pull the truck out of its muddy bath and they got on their way.

We can choose how we respond to an obstacle. Like the three men, our response may be to curse and give up, to sit back and wait for someone else to help us, or to set to work fearlessly to try to overcome it ourselves. The event itself isn't important; how we think about it is.

Is there an obstacle in my way today?

*The most useless day of all is that in
which we have not laughed.*
—*Sebastian R. N. Champort*

We are told that laughter is sunshine filling a
room. And where there is laughter, there also is
life. They say that people who laugh a lot live
longer than do the sour-faced. When we laugh together, gratitude comes more easily, companion-
ship thrives, and all praise is sincere. Laughter
brings us joy that cannot be bought. Such joy is
with us throughout each day. To hoard joy, to hide
it away deep within us away from others, will
make us lonely misers. We cannot buy or trade for
joy, but we can give or receive it as a gift.

Laughter's joy celebrates the moment we are living right now. It is a gift we must share, or it will
wither and die. Shared, it grows and thrives, and
always returns to us when we need it most.

What can I find to laugh about right now?

February 26

> *From harmony, from heavenly*
> *harmony,*
> *This universal frame began. . . .*
> —*John Dryden*

Our family is like a small orchestra. Each of us has an important part to play. To achieve harmony we tune in to how others are sounding.   We recognize that every orchestra needs a conductor, a center for direction. We rely on our Higher Power for this support and guidance, and we realize that our family's music exists in time. It changes, it passes, and we begin a new song. Our music comes and goes. It is not carved in marble. It is a free expression of family love.

No one of us has to play alone, because we are an ensemble. The time for soloing comes later. Today we rejoice that we can play together.

How can my music add to the family's symphony today?

*The great pleasure in life is doing what
people say you cannot do.*
                    —Walter Babehot

Everyone knew Jacob was a bitter, old hermit
who hated people. He lived by himself in a cabin
in the woods. He never came to town, never talked
to anyone, and never put up a mailbox or put in a
phone. But he had one thing the townsfolk wanted
— the very first Bible brought by a preacher when
the town was first settled. They wanted it for their
centennial celebration.

Little Tom listened as the townsfolk complained
daily about how much they wanted the old book
to put on display. One day, he walked on out to the
little cabin and just asked the old man if he could
borrow the book, just for a week. Imagine the
surprise on the faces of the people when the boy
wandered back to town with the old dusty book in
hand.

Are we like the townspeople sometimes? Do we
assume things won't work out without even trying? Sometimes help is there, just waiting to be
asked. What have we got to lose?

*What can I request today that I have been afraid to
ask for?*

February 28

> *Nothing that is worth doing can be done alone, but has to be done with others.*
> —*Dr. Reinhold Niebuhr*

We who are blessed with a closely-knit family life, where thoughts and actions can be discussed and developed, are aware that what is given is not as important as what is shared. As we help one another, we learn that sharing can never exist unless we care first. This is the major ingredient of love.

Albert Schweitzer described human service toward a common goal as the greatest of deeds. Charles Dickens assured us that when we lighten the burdens of another, we can never consider ourselves useless. Those of us who are led today may show the way tomorrow. In giving, we receive, and in getting we cannot avoid being givers.

What do I receive by giving today?

Belief consists in accepting the affirmations of the soul; unbelief, in denying them.
—*Ralph Waldo Emerson*

What do we believe? Do we believe in ourselves? Do we believe we have enough time and energy to do what we need? Or do we believe that things will turn out badly for us? Someone said that fear is faith in the negative. We can choose to believe the worst will happen, or we can choose to believe we deserve good things. We can believe the right things will happen at the right time. What we believe becomes true for us because we behave as though it were true. For this reason, it is wise to choose our beliefs carefully. The more we choose the positive, the more aware we become that our choices are many.

This means telling ourselves that we're all right just as we are, and acting as though it were true without question.

How can I make my world better today?

March

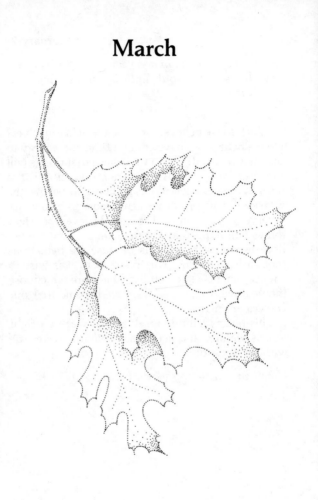

*The only thing that makes life possible
is permanent, intolerable uncertainly:
not knowing what comes next.*
                    —Ursula LeGuin

The world around us changes constantly. Trees turn from green to beautiful shades of yellow, orange and brown in the fall. Yet, even if we watch the trees carefully, every minute of the day, we could not actually see the colors change. Change requires time, preparation, and patience.

To make the changes we want, we need to let go of unhealthy but comfortable patterns that we're stuck in, the way the trees let their colors change, and finally let go of their leaves altogether. We can't have total change right now, no matter how much we want it. It's important to accept both who we are now and who we are becoming. Just as the tree trusts without question that its leaves will grow, and lets go of them when the time comes, we can believe in our own power to grow, and let go of our accomplishments when the time is right.

When we do, we can be assured that our lives will blossom again, like trees in the spring, coming to life after a cold winter.

Do I have any new blossoms today?

March 2

> *I was angry with my friend:*
> *I told my wrath, my wrath did end.*
> *I was angry with my foe:*
> *I told it not, no wrath did grow.*
> —*William Blake*

We have a right to claim our own feelings. Sometimes we get angry, but hold it inside because we think it's wrong to feel it. If anger builds inside us, it expands like a balloon ready to burst. If not released, it can make us depressed, or even physically ill. When we give ourselves permission to feel anger, we are better able to get rid of it in a healthy way. Our inner voice can tell us how to let go of our anger. And once we've released it, we can easily get in touch with the feelings that caused it.

When we recognize our anger for what it is — one feeling among many others that makes us unique — it loses its significance, and we can prevent it from consuming us. Indira Ghandi said, "You cannot shake hands with a clenched fist." When we let go of our anger we can honestly embrace each other with open arms.

Am I carrying around anger which could be released today?

Nothing is troublesome that we do willingly.
                                    —Thomas Jefferson

Some of the necessary things we do are tiring and annoying. Many of these things we must do regardless of how we feel about them. Doing dishes day after day can be a tiresome job but, no matter how much we hate it, it must be done sooner or later. We might discover, if we look hard enough, how chores like this can actually be enjoyable, if we do them right. Perhaps dish washing is a time for listening to music and singing along, or an opportunity for conversation between family members as we help one another.

Our willingness to look for the hidden treasure and opportunities in tasks we might otherwise consider dreary will never fail to reward us.

What opportunity can I see in my next chore?

March 4

*I celebrate myself, and sing myself, and
what I assume, you shall assume.*
                                        —Walt Whitman

Some of us may think Walt Whitman must have
been terribly conceited to have written words like
that. But he wasn't. He knew himself well, and
accepted himself, even his darker side. He could
laugh at himself and celebrate his humanness.

And because he loved and accepted himself just
as he was, others could do the same. That's difficult to understand sometimes, but it's true: no one
else is going to love and accept us until we come to
love and accept ourselves.

We teach others how to treat us by the way we
treat ourselves, so perhaps it makes sense to apply
a variation of the Golden Rule: "Do unto ourselves
as we would have others do unto us."

*Can I allow my kindness to myself overflow to
another person today?*

*The farmer may only be planting a
seed, but if he opens his eyes he is feed-
ing the whole world.*
—*Omaha Bee*

A traveller journeying through a small village
came upon some workers building an impressive
structure. "What are you doing?" he asked. The
first worker, a young, impatient man, replied in
disgust, "I am making three dollars an hour and
getting very tired!" The visitor asked another man
the same question. "I'm mixing concrete, as you
can plainly see," came the sarcastic reply. Finally, a
woman working nearby left her wheelbarrow full
of bricks and approached the stranger. "We are
building a hospital," she said with pride. "Now we
will be able to care for all the region's people. Babies will be born here. Lives will be saved."

The stranger looked at the woman with admiration and spoke directly to her. "I know, for this is
my hospital. Only you hold the vision of what it is
you are creating." The wealthy benefactor then put
the woman in charge of construction so his hospital would be built by one who truly understood.

*Will I see the true importance of even the small
things I do today?*

March 6

*This Mouse must give up one of his
Mouse ways of seeing things in order
that he may grow.*
　　　　　　　—Hyemeyohsts Storm

There is an American Indian tale of a mouse
who heard a roaring in his ears and set out to
discover what it was. He encountered many animals who helped him on his way. Finally, the
mouse had a chance to offer help to another. He
gave away his eyes to help two other animals.

Without his sight, defenseless, he waited for the
end. Soon he heard the sound eagles make when
they dive for their prey. The next thing the mouse
knew, he was flying. He could see all the splendor
around him. Then he heard a voice say, "You have
a new name. You are Eagle."

Like the mouse, we also feel something inside us
we'd like to explore. That secret, like all others,
has its answer hidden deep within us, yet right
under our very noses. Often, we merely have to
give up our eyes and see in a different way. When
we do this, we are rewarded with a new kind of
vision, one that lets us discover our true potential.

How can I look at things differently today?

*He who distributes the milk of human
kindness cannot help but spill a little on
himself.*

—*James Barrie*

We like ourselves best when we like those
around us. When we smile at them, they smile
back; when we ask them, they tell us about themselves. When we scowl at people, they'll frown
back; when we ignore them, they'll walk away.

It's true that we get back what we put into
things, whether it's work, play, love, or gardening.
We decide by the extent of our commitment how
valuable or enjoyable or depressing an experience
can be for us.

Our actions toward others come right back to
us. When we smile at people, they smile back, and
we feel good. Sometimes feeling good about ourselves depends on feeling good about others.
When we send out that smile of ours, those who
get it pass it on, and we have added power to the
happiness of this world.

*What can I do to show my fondness for others
today?*

March 8

Laughter by definition is healthy.
                    —Doris Lessing

A hearty laugh can warm a cold room and make our spirits soar. But many of us are afraid to laugh, especially when we make mistakes. We think we're supposed to be perfect, and we don't allow ourselves to make mistakes. However, we're not a mold punched out by a machine. We're human beings, with all our wonderful flaws. It is those flaws that make our lives interesting and surprising. Who knows when we might accidentally bump into a chair or catch our sweater on a doorknob? We needn't feel self-conscious, it happens to many of us.

The ability to laugh at ourselves is a gift from God. All we need to do is grab it and use it. Then we will see how healthy and powerful laughter can be.

Can I find the humor in my mistakes today?

There is no such thing as a long piece of work, except one that you dare not start.

—Charles Baudelaire

A big assignment can be scary to face. We may start to think that how we do on the assignment will determine if we're good or bad people. The more we think about it, the harder that task seems. The key to overcoming our negative feelings is to say to ourselves that we are capable of finishing our projects. We must say it over and over until we start believing it's true. Then we can attack the assignment with vitality and positive energy we didn't know we had.

We can make up our minds to do our best and accept that from ourselves. No one is perfect. We live in a world full of wonderful devices created by people just like ourselves. We say Edison was a genius, but our lightbulbs still burn out regularly. Even Einstein was wrong once in a while, and he knew it, but that didn't stop him from trying.

When we feel afraid to start something because it seems too big a job, let's stop and think what the first step would be, and do each small step in its own time.

What can I start that I've been putting off?

March 10

> *The older you get the more you realize*
> *that kindness is synonymous with hap-*
> *piness.*
>
> *—Lionel Barrymore*

Once in a while, we forget about the kind things people have done for us. Do we remember the next door neighbor who helped us get our kite out of a tree, or the brother who helped us finish a project for school? If we think about these kindnesses, we will remember how happy we were to receive them.

These people and others may need a kindness we can give. Our next door neighbor may get sick and need us to go to the store, a brother or sister may need to borrow a radio, or the elderly person down the street may need the lawn mowed. Whenever we take the time to give a kindness, we will find, like the boomerang, it returns to us in the form of happiness.

Will I be alert to my chances to give kindness to-day?

*Being a healthy parent means being
firm but nurturing, giving children a
decent sense of the boundaries along
with lots of unconditional love.*
　　　　　　　　　—Karen Shaud

In a healthy family, life goes along and everybody pitches in to do the housework. Some people
wonder why housework is such a big deal. It is
because people need to contribute to a group in
order to feel they belong to it. Housework makes
us part of the same group — our house, our family. We make our house comfortable so we can feel
comfortable and safe in it. We show love for ourselves by making our surroundings likeable. And
when we do physical work, we can do our inner
housekeeping, letting go of negative feelings that
pile up during the day.

On days when life feels out of control, we feel
good when we do one simple job: clean the messy
desk, wash dirty dishes, shovel the snowy walk. In
this way we regain control of our feelings as well
as a perspective on those things within our control.

*What simple work do I need to do to feel better
today?*

March 12

Gentleness is not a quality exclusive to women.

—Helen Reddy

Each of us has our soft side; maybe it's when we're petting a kitten, caring for a baby robin with an injured wing, or soothing a crying child who is afraid. Behaving in a gentle way toward others gives us warm feelings inside. It also encourages others to treat us gently, too.

We don't always feel like being gentle. If we're sad, or worried about school or a friend, we might not even notice the people around us who need our gentleness. But when we remember gentleness, it lifts our spirits. Two people will always be happier when we're gentle — the person we've been gentle to and ourselves.

Who can I share my gentleness with today?

*I never dreamed of so much happiness
when I was the ugly duckling.*
        —Hans Christian Anderson

The ugly duckling was not really ugly at all, he was just different. The other ducks teased and pecked and even bit him until the ugly duckling flew away. He wandered around for a year, and was treated as an outcast everywhere. In the spring, he saw a group of swans on a lake, and wanted very much to join them. As he swam out toward them, he was astounded to notice his reflection in the water — he was a swan! The other swans welcomed him warmly, and found him to be beautiful.

Most of us go through times when we feel different from those around us. These are painful and lonely times, but it doesn't mean there is anything wrong with us. Like the ugly duckling, we will come into a time when we will be loved. All the pain and loneliness we have felt will help us fully appreciate the acceptance when we find it.

How can I treasure the ways I am different from others today?

March 14

Each man with a new idea is a crank
until the idea succeeds.
— *Mark Twain*

What does it mean to be different? How does it feel? Is it okay to act or look or be different from everyone else at times? Sometimes, maybe even most of the time, it feels safer to blend into the crowd. We don't want to stick out like a sore thumb. But sometimes it's when we are different that we discover new things no one has ever thought of or done before.

We don't want to spend our whole lives doing only what others do. And there are times when we must take a stand if what others are doing is wrong. Perhaps it's good practice to try to do some little thing differently once in a while, to stand out from the crowd, just to get used to it. We might even like it. After all, if no one ever dares to be different, how would our world ever change for the better?

What little thing can I do to stand out from the crowd today?

The difficulty in life is the choice.
　　　　　　　—George Moore

How we choose to spend our time says much about what is important to us. If we have no goals, we may try to kill time. If we have too many goals, there may not be enough time in the day to do all we set out to do. We must make some choices based on our values. We may need to take more time for some things, and let go of others. For example, this year will we try to learn to play the guitar? Perhaps we have finally decided to drop out of that club which seems to have little purpose. Will we give more time to work, or less time? With each of these choices, we shape our lives. We can do it with the touch of an artist if we pay attention to the choices we are making.

What is truly important to me today?

March 16

'Tis God gives skill, but not without men's hands: He could not make Antonio Stradivarius violins without Antonio.

—George Eliot

When she was four years old, she climbed onto the piano stool and, to her parents' astonishment, a simple prelude she'd heard on the radio flew across the keys from her fingers. That very week they found her a teacher, and the house was filled with the music of her developing talent.

While other girls played, made the honor roll, starred on the basketball team, and dated boyfriends, she sat inside at her beloved piano and practiced. At seventeen, when she made her debut, the critics said, "She's a natural. A genius!"

We know she was no natural, but through hard work, she made her piano playing part of her nature. When we put love into our labor, our own dreams grow into being.

Am I willing to make some sacrifices today to do the things I really want to do?

Love is always open arms.
                    —Leo Buscaglia

There is a story about a boy who left home and dishonored his father by spending a large amount of money in fast and reckless living. When the boy's money ran out, he was faced with the prospect of returning home to face his father, knowing the father had every reason to be disappointed in him. Filled with fear and shame he approached his home, his mind racing with words of apology. Before the boy could say a word, his father rushed to him with open arms and hugged his lost son in joy and love.

Have we done this? Have we found it in our hearts to approve whatever a loved one does, even if we would have wanted something different?

Love like this is the highest kind of love. It finds joy in others no matter what, because it recognizes the freedom of those we love, and doesn't chain them to our own wants. It is the same kind of love God has for us.

Are my arms open today?

March 18

Tyger, Tyger, burning bright,
In the forests of the night;
What immortal hand or eye,
Could frame thy fearful symmetry?
Did He who made the Lamb
 make thee?

—William Blake

Is there both a lamb and a tiger inside us? Is there any commandment, written on the sky or a stone tablet, denying us our perfect right to be both tiger and lamb? The tiger, beast made of fire and night, shows its teeth when it blazes with love; the lamb, orphan wrapped in soft blanket of cloud, weeps to receive that same love. So we give and take, are strong and weak, guilty and innocent, wrong and right. So we are balanced, even when we seem to be in conflict.

When we learn to accept all the things we can be, we will be able to love all the ways the world outside us can be.

What conflict is helping me grow today?

Where is the yesterday that worried us so?

—*Joan Walsh Anglund*

In the fairy tale *The Last Dream of the Old Oak Tree*, the oak tree felt sorry for the day-fly. The day-fly only lives for one day, and the tree was already 365 years old. But the day-fly was so enjoying his one day that the tree's sympathy puzzled him. The day-fly said to the tree, "You may have thousands of my days, but I have thousands of moments to be pleased and happy in."

And so the day-fly continued to dance in the sun and smell the clover and honeysuckle. His day ended as happily as he spent it, settling down on a blade of grass.

If all of us could approach our day the way the day-fly does, as though this were our only day, we would spend less time worrying about yesterday and tomorrow.

How can I show my gratitude for the gift of this day?

March 20

I want, by understanding myself, to understand others.
        —*Katherine Mansfield*

Growing up to be the best people we can be is a lifelong process. As teenagers, we may have thought that twenty-one would be a magic year for us because then we would become adults. We'd be grown up and able to handle easily any problems that came along, if any did.

But the older we get, the more we realize that growing up is a process that never ends. We are always becoming the people we are capable of being. We're always learning new things about ourselves, and in that process we're always coming to new understandings about other people and how we can get along with them.

How wonderful that life always offers us room to grow! It makes new discoveries possible all through our lives, and ensures us that we will always have something to offer.

What discovery have I made just today?

Humpty Dumpty sat on a wall,
Humpty Dumpty had a great fall.
　　　　　—Mother Goose

Poor Humpty ended up such a scrambled egg. Maybe that's what comes from sitting too long in one place, choosing neither this way nor that, playing both sides against the middle. Maybe he played too much politics, got too much advice, had too much to think about. When the centipede was asked which leg he first moved when setting out on a stroll, he got those legs all tangled in his mind and couldn't walk at all. It is better to be simply moved by those around us, or our Higher Power, with faith and love. When our thoughts fail, their hearts, hands, and eyes will show the way.

Do I sometimes decide my fate by refusing to decide?

March 22

Real men don't vacuum.
—Anna Genich

Once, not so long ago, there was a family who tried to divide up housework equally. The father signed up for vacuuming, but he never got around to doing it.

One morning he told everyone about his dream the night before. He was lined up in the dining room with an entire football team, and they all ran in a line through the house, pushing the clutter and dirt up against the walls and out of the way. They came to a finish at the picture window, where the father turned and raised his arms in victory. Then he saw his wife watching him, so he explained, "Heroes don't vacuum."

Perhaps each of us is a hero at one time or another. In that case, we might take turns at different chores, rewarding the day's hero with a day off from vacuuming or dishwashing. When we work together to get the chores done, we become a family of heroes, and can feel a healthy pride in our warm, loving, and clean home.

How can we share housework more equally?

It feels so good to cry. . .
                                    —Susan Cygnet

Some of us were taught that it's bad to express our feelings directly — crying, wailing, jumping up and down for joy, that it's good manners to always talk softly, slowly, and politely and to sit still.

But what happens to our feelings when we sit still? If they don't get expressed, they must be caught inside our bodies. Trapped feelings are like birds in a cage, or a rabbit in a trap, they try to get out any way they can. They peck on our heads and give us headaches. They scratch at our stomachs and make us hurt.

We must let them out. We must laugh and cry. Then our bodies will be happy, and our feelings will curl up in our laps like happy puppies.

Am I ignoring the physical symptoms of trapped feelings?

March 24

The things we hate about ourselves aren't more real than things we like about ourselves.

—Ellen Goodman

It is so easy, and tempting, to get down on ourselves, to focus on an imperfect face, a dismal batting average, our fear of math, or our big feet. The trouble is, the more we feel sorry for ourselves, the more we have to feel sorry about. And though it probably doesn't hurt to indulge in a little self-pity once in a while, how unfortunate — and limiting — it can be to let those attitudes define us.

The things we hate about ourselves are no more real than the things we like about ourselves. The trick is to dwell on the things we like instead of those we don't. Even on days when we are sure we are the least loveable creatures in the world, we can *act as if* we like ourselves. What a surprise, at the end of the day, to find out that we actually do!

What can I like about myself today?

*My most irrational fear is that I've for-
gotten how to cook.*
                                    —*Pam Sherman*

Once there was a teacher who was having night-
mares about doing a good job. In one dream, he
couldn't find his classroom and he had to run from
building to building. In another dream, he started
teaching the lesson in the middle of the woods and
didn't notice he was in the wrong place!

Then, one Sunday morning, he read an article
about a wonderful baker. She baked every day,
started bakeries, fixed food for her friends, yet
when the reporter asked her about her fears, she
said, "My most irrational fear is that I've forgotten
how to cook."

Suddenly the man felt better. He realized someone else had the same kinds of fears. In a miraculous way, our fears become less powerful when we
discover that we share them with other people.

What fear can I share with someone right now?

March 26

There is a proper balance between not asking enough of oneself and asking or expecting too much.

—*May Sarton*

The boy's mother baked pies that morning before he was up. She left them on the back porch to cool, their warm aroma curling up through his bedroom window. His mouth was full of the smell when he woke.

Before she left for work, she said, "You may do anything you want today, anything at all. Except for one thing — don't step in those pies."

All day the boy could not get the pies out of his mind; his feet itched just thinking about them.

Don't step in those pies. He heard her voice inside his head. By late afternoon he could control it no longer. One, two, three, four, five, six — his foot fell squarely into the middle of each pie.

When we expect the worst from others, we often get just that. The same goes for our expectations of ourselves. And when we trust others, it, too, is returned.

Do I expect the best of others — and myself — today?

*We like someone because, we love
someone although.*
　　　　　—Henri de Montherlant

Families are like scissors. They are joined in the
middle but often spread wide apart, moving away
from each other. When we're not feeling close to
other family members — when it's hard to even
like them — it seems like we'll never come together
again.

But pity the scrap of paper that comes between
our scissor blades! The scissors works together
again and slices the trouble clean. When trouble
threatens our family, we can slice it through if we
move together in love and acceptance.

No matter our small differences, we are part of
the same living organism, in a way. The family we
live in has been together for many generations, and
we are just the most recent members. When we
look at one another, we see the products of centuries of love.

*When I feel distant from my family, can I locate
where we are still joined together?*

March 28

> *I have a feeling I should paint what I am supposed to paint. So I sit. And there my hand moves and I made a picture.*
>
> —Norval Morrijeau

The writer sits, head in hands, amid a mound of crumpled paper wads. The deadline is tomorrow and not even the first paragraph is written. The writer has been working nonstop since the early morning hours. Frustration pushes the writer up from the chair and out on a long walk in the woods to the stream. After an hour of plunging through lush woods, a rest by the stream listening to the sounds of the rippling water is refreshing. Back at the typewriter, the fingers move, the words flow, the job is done.

Sometimes we need to quiet ourselves to let our inner resources flow through our outer noise. We are always doing what we are supposed to do. Even when things don't seem to come together just right, there is a purpose, even if only to let us know we need to do something else for a while.

How much simpler our lives can be if we only have the faith to accept what happens as a guidepost along a path that is naturally correct.

Am I frustrated with something I should step away from?

*Drag your thoughts away from your
troubles . . . by the ears, by the heels or
any other way you can manage it. It's
the healthiest thing a body can do.*
                                    —Mark Twain

It requires very little effort — and no imagination — to start feeling sorry for ourselves. Often, it
is easy to feel sorry for ourselves in our families.
Instead of being inspired by the sports talents of an
older brother, the popularity of a lovely sister, or
the fame of a parent or relative, we often take the
easier attitude: "I'm denied all that he or she has."

If we work hard at developing our own abilities
so that we can excel, we will find ourselves proud
of, and applauding, what others do. If a personal
problem brings us self-pity, we must remind ourselves that all people also have problems. We can
cope as well as the best of people if we learn from
them and think positively.

*Who among those close to me can I be proud of
today?*

March 30

Come stand by my side where
  I'm going,
Take my hand if I stumble and fall
It's the strength that you share when
  you're growing
That gives me what I need
  most of all.

—Hoyt Axton

The bear cub was miserable. Her father, the leader of the pack, had left a month ago to find them winter shelter and had not yet returned. Everyone went on as if nothing had changed.

One evening the cub had a dream in which her father appeared and said, "Daughter, I know you grieve for me, but your burden is too heavy to carry alone. Share it with the others and let them comfort you. Sharing will only lighten your load and if you can accept help now you will find it easier to give when others are in need."

The next morning the little cub woke with a much lighter heart. As it turns out, everyone in the pack shared the same dream. There was much hugging and crying and reaching out and healing.

We can easily lighten our loads by asking support from those who love us, knowing our turn to help will come.

What help can I ask for today?

Withdrawal is a preparation for emergence.

—Nor Hall

A man lost his family in a car accident and wanted to be alone for a while, but he worried whether he was doing the right thing. Then one day a friend told him that when pine cones fall off the Lodge Pole Pine trees, they are sealed shut so the seeds inside can't get out. The pine cones lie on the forest floor — sometimes for decades — until a forest fire sweeps through. Heat from the fire melts the seal and the seeds fall out and finally grow, and that's why the Lodge Pole Pine is called a *fire origin species.*

The man felt good about himself when he heard the story. *Fire origin species* is a good name for people who've been burned by life and find new growth as a result.

How have I grown because of pain and difficulty?

April

Then Bacchus. . .gave him the choice of making a wish come true. . . . So Midas said, "Make everything I touch turn gold."

—*Ovid*

Poor King Midas, already rich as a king, was made poorer by his poor wish. Everything he touched — small shoots, wet clay, a ripe head of wheat, apples from a tree — all suddenly went bad, turned into gold, pure gold. And how could he eat when bread and fruits, even fresh running water, suddenly shined at him, yellow, hard, and cold? He could have wished for a wiser, smaller success. He could have had all familiar things turn kind at his touch, or loving and good. Then imagine how he would have touched everyone he came near.

If some wishes are too good to be true, are others too bad?

April 2

It is wealth to be content.

—Lao-tzu

On the evening of the first day of spring, a woman gave her husband a bright red geranium in a clay pot. To celebrate, he placed it on the window sill, and together they marvelled at the delicate petals.

In the harsher light of morning, though, the man frowned at the geranium and said to his wife, "How shabby it makes the sofa look." They spent the day at the furniture store and came home with a new couch, blue with red flowers, like the geranium. They placed the couch in front of the window sill and admired together its grace and line and fashionable upholstery.

But the next morning, the man frowned at the couch and said, "How shabby it makes the carpet look." Soon they had a lavish new carpet, which led to new curtains, lamps, and chairs. When the room was completely redone, they set the geranium back in the window and surveyed the finest room in the neighborhood. The man frowned. "The geranium," he said, "it's out of place. It will have to go."

Will I be able to appreciate life's simple pleasures today?

> *If there is anything we wish to change
> in the child, we should first examine it
> and see whether it is not something that
> could be better changed in ourselves.*
> —*Carl Jung*

Children are smart. Remember how we used to imitate our parents' behavior? We'd dress up like them, mimic their words, even copy their attitudes. We wanted to be just like them because we thought they were the most wonderful people in the world. We can see this happen all around us, younger ones imitating parents, older brothers and sisters, and older friends. It's very flattering.

The problem is that children imitate not just healthy behavior and attitudes, but also sometimes the not-so-healthy. We get very uncomfortable when we look at a younger person misbehaving and see ourselves in that person. Suddenly, we aren't flattered any more.

When we see things we don't like in others, we must first look at ourselves to see if we need changing. This is all we can do — change ourselves. Others may follow our example or they may not, but we can be sure that, when we watch our own behavior, most of what we see of ourselves in others will be flattering.

What change can I make in myself to set a good example today?

April 4

One day at a time — this is enough. Do not look back and grieve over the past, for it is gone.

—Ida Scott Taylor

It's not always easy to understand that the day stretching before us is all that counts. Daydreaming about the party last week, or getting upset all over again about a fight we had yesterday with a friend doesn't help us right now. When our minds are on the past, we miss out on the conversation or the activity that is going on around us.

Every moment of the day is special, and guaranteed to help us grow and understand life. All of us have been taught to pay attention in school, or to pay attention when others talk to us. But we should also pay attention to the birds, the sky, even the grass. And we can learn a lot by paying attention to the conversations going on around us, and to the small voice inside us that helps us know right from wrong.

What's going on today is enough to pay attention to.

Am I ready to pay attention to what is around me today?

I measure every Grief I meet
With narrow, probing, Eyes —
I wonder if it weighs like Mine —
Or has an easier size.
                    —Emily Dickinson

How can we measure all the grief we feel, and how can we put up with it? Doesn't the Grief of Death weigh a ton or more? Doesn't it stretch out to a month, a year, or longer still? Is the Grief of Failure lighter than the Grief of Despair, but maybe longer? Isn't the Grief of Emptiness the heaviest of all? Whether we try to ignore or make light of it, our grief, like a ton of feathers or a ton of rocks, is all the same to us. This much is sure: if we lock our grief in, it will weigh more on us and lengthen out; if we open our hearts with weeping and words, others will help carry it away.

What old sadness can I let go of by sharing it today?

April 6

In quarreling about the shadow, we often lose the substance.

—Aesop

There is a fable about a man and his camel who were hired by a wealthy man to get him across the desert. The journey was so hot that they stopped to rest one day, and the only shade to be found was in the shadow of the camel. The two of them began to argue about who had the rights to the camel's shadow — the owner or the renter. They were so involved in their argument that the camel ran away and they didn't notice until it was long gone.

Sometimes we get so caught up in being right that we become like these two, fighting over a shadow. Instead of paying attention to our journey and sharing what we have, we let ourselves get distracted. It is more important to notice what we have, to share it as best we can, and continue our journey.

What can I share with another today?

*Take time every day to do something
silly.*
> —*Philipa Walker*

Spring fever may bring out our longings and our
sense of unfilled needs for attention, play, or
laughter. We may be afraid to express these needs
because they are not often taken seriously, but
thought of as childish. We may even be afraid our
needs are so enormous that they will never be satisfied, and so we keep them bottled up inside ourselves, and all we can express to others is frustration.

Spring is a reminder that we can find a way to
satisfy our needs. We can give ourselves a break
from work or study, laugh a little, and try to share
our laughter with someone else. There are many
ways to fulfill a need, and by giving what we have
to offer, we may find ourselves getting back exactly what we really need, even though it may not
be what we had hoped for.

In the act of giving we learn we are worth giving
to, also. We learn that we deserve to be loved,
most of all by ourselves.

What do I think I need today?

April 8

Any time you sense you are getting overrun by outside influences and losing your feelings, put your attention inside your body. Relax. . ., let your breath sink low. . ., breathe in your abdomen. . . .

—Anne Kent Rush

When we are feeling as though all our energy is scattered throughout our bodies, we need to practice centering, or focusing this energy into one place. Our center may change from day to day, and each of us feels it differently.

When we're walking, we may feel power coming from our hips and spreading through the body, heart, and mind. When we're in a meditative mood, we may feel warm energy at the back of the head. At other times, we might feel a real centering place in the middle of the chest, right where our hearts and arms and breathing come together.

There is no one way to be at peace. Centering is a way for each of us to find and picture to ourselves our focused energy. When we can do this, we increase our power to bring about those things we want from life, those things we really do deserve.

Where is my energy right now?

There are persons who have some parts like me, but no one adds up exactly like me.

—*Virginia Satir*

Most of us feel pretty ordinary. We probably wish we were taller or shorter. Some of us are fat rather than thin. Few of us have perfect skin or teeth. Often we look at others, compare ourselves, and wish we were different. At these times, it's important to remember that each of us is special. We differ from others because we're created for different purposes.

Some of us will make a contribution to the world of sports, some to the art of music. Teaching or medicine will attract others and yet, no two of us will give to the world in the same way. Our unique mixture of looks, attitudes, and abilities will be special and very necessary to the people sharing our lifetime.

How can I give my special gift to the world today?

April 10

But don't go into Mr. McGregor's garden.

—Beatrix Potter

Since we are members of a family, we are not free to do anything we like. We may not be able to go as far from home as we would like. We may have to get up earlier in the morning than we would like. We may have only limited use of the car. Families set up limits in order to maintain order and happiness. If each of us demanded something different for supper each night, the situation would be unmanageable.

Limits also keep us safe. When Peter Rabbit was told not to go into Mr. McGregor's garden, it was for his own good. Limits and restrictions are a form of love and protection, and we all have them. When we bump up against one of these limits, we can be assured they serve to point us in another direction, one with freedoms of its own which we may never have explored without being forced to.

What freedom can I discover in a limitation today?

*Listen to your feelings. They tell you
when you need to take care of yourself,
like finding a friend if you feel lonely,
crying if you feel sad, singing and smiling if you feel happy, and acting frisky
if you feel good.*

—*Pat Palmer*

When we get too much of anything — too much
fun or too much work — we may feel really
crummy when it's over.

One way to listen to our crummy feelings is to
say, "Here comes the letdown after all that fun."
We can imagine a spaceship falling to earth, float-
ing on the ocean. Coming down to earth is as
much a part of the adventure as the countdown
and blastoff.

A letdown for us means we need to let our
bodies and minds rest, just like the spaceship, bob-
bing around without any special direction. We
need to take it easy, do nothing, put off making
plans.

Then we can ask God to help us let go of the
crummy feelings that come along with a letdown.
We can ask the spirit within us to guide us through
this time of change. Then we will let down and let
go.

*What are some things I can do to take it easy the
next time I feel down?*

April 12

*I come into the peace of wild things
who do not tax their lives with fore-
thought of grief.*
                                    —*Wendell Berry*

Blessed are all birds and animals, the wildest beasts, and, yes, all serpents, too, for they live in nature, in a state of natural grace. They live beyond the rules of evil and good. Their instincts are obedient only to the laws of survival, growth, and health. And as their lives unfurl in obedience to these laws, they suffer no shame, regret, or sin. Nor do they curse their failures, or themselves.

We can learn much from them. They harbor no evil toward one another, and they trust their own inner sense of how to live, and that their Higher Power makes sure everything which befalls them is for the best. Yes, they are blessed, and so are we, the highest animal.

What guilt can I free myself from today, just by letting go?

Nobody can be in good health if he does not have all the time fresh air, sunshine, and good water.
—Chief Flying Hawk

Before this part of the world was colonized by Europeans, native Americans thrived here, living in wigwams and teepees, spending their time in the fresh air and sun, and drinking pure, fresh water from springs, streams, and rivers. They lived long, healthy lives and almost never were sick — precisely because they knew how important the natural elements were.

When we feel depressed or nervous, nature is a good listener. We can take a walk in the sun, listen to the small birds, or twigs cracking under our feet, or simply the sound of our shoes on the pavement.

We don't need to live in teepees to follow the Indians' example today. But getting out in the sunshine and fresh air every day, even on really cold days, rejuvenates us. Sunlight is healing, fresh air cleanses our lungs and brings more oxygen to the blood and brain. When we think enough of ourselves to take a walk when we need it, even that small amount of self-consideration is also healing.

Have I given myself time to live outside today?

April 14

There the penitents took off their shoes
And walked barefoot the remaining
  mile.
                              —Robert Lowell

Some people have to have pain. If dirt doesn't
fall on their heads from the sky, they sulk in corners and hope their flesh turns to dust. They do
everything the hard way, even when they know
better, and often complain and accuse others for
their pain. For people like this, even the song of a
bird is a bother. It's better to smile when people
like that accuse. It's better to wear shoes when
walking on stones, better to take the shortest way.
There is weeping and wailing enough in the world,
dumps full of worn-out guilt and remorse. When
the bird sings, it's better to look up and see that it
beats its wings not to punish itself, but to fly.

Do I pity myself when I could be flying?

If I have freedom in my love,
And in my soul am free,
Angels alone that soar above
Enjoy such liberty.
                            —*Richard Lovelace*

When a cow decides to stop nursing her calf, she isn't rejecting it. She knows it's time for the calf to be on its own. Although the calf might feel rejected and puzzled at first, it soon adapts to its new independence and freedom.

When we feel rejected, it's useful to remember that whatever has caused us to feel this way might have nothing to do with us. It might be a reflection of what's happening with someone else, or just the end of a natural stage in life, as with the calf.

When we understand that others' actions toward us come from their own feelings, and that we don't cause their feelings any more than they control ours, we can free ourselves from a little bit of fear and self-hate. We can see what seems to be rejection as an open door, with our freedom on the other side.

What rejections have set me free?

April 16

*. . .there is as much dignity in tilling a
field as in writing a poem.*
                    —Booker T. Washington

It's not what we do for a job that counts, it's
how we do it. It's not what our chores at home
might be, it's how we do them. And it's not what
grades we get in school, but rather how hard we
try. Doing our best, whether it's making a bed,
writing a report, or listening to a friend tell about
an experience gives us a good feeling about ourselves.

Each of us is special to one another. And we are
special to this very moment. Because what is past
can't be repeated, let's remember to enjoy every
moment as it comes. Let's pay close attention to
each person, each activity that we encounter today. It's not what we do today, but how we do it
that counts.

*Can I do each thing well today, even the small
things?*

*If your heart catches in your throat ask
a bird how she sings.*
                              —*Cooper Edens*

The idea of your heart getting caught in your throat and then asking a bird how she sings may seem silly. It is, but being silly is sometimes exactly what we need. Instead of always trying to figure out the lumps in our throats, we can learn how to sing with it.

Birds sing all day. Their songs are lighthearted and playful. And they bring us color along with their songs. We have all stopped to notice a special bird outside the window. A bird song can be a lullaby. It can be laughter. We need these things in our lives, too. By playing and laughing, we change the lumps in our throats to songs.

What sadness can I turn into song today?

April 18

Gifts are for giving.
— *Ian and Sylvia Tyson*

Many years ago, a young woman named Dorothy was very talented at china painting. She painted tiny scenes on china dishes, the way people today paint on wood and Easter eggs.

Then Dorothy fell in love, got married, and decided she had no time to paint. But as her children grew, they loved to stand at the china cabinet and stare at all her tiny pictures — each one seemed to hold its own special world.

Years passed, and Dorothy's grandchildren also loved to stand and stare at the paintings. Everybody loved her work. They wondered why she didn't take up painting again, but she wouldn't say. Her love of painting seemed to be locked away.

When we give up some talent of our own because we don't have time for it, we lock away part of ourselves. When we imprison our talents, we limit our possibilities. But when we make self-expression a natural part of our day, others can gather around and enjoy the results. There is always room for our talents because they create worlds of their own.

Am I locking something away because I don't have the time?

Inch by inch, row by row
Someone bless these seeds I sow. . .
'Til the rain comes tumblin' down.
                    —David Mallett

We plant a garden with faith, never knowing exactly what the harvest will bring. We attend to those aspects of gardening which we have some control over, planting good seeds in rich soil, in straight rows, the right distance apart. We weed and fertilize, and we tie up our tomato plants.

We may pray for rain, but we never know if we'll get too much or too little. We can't control the wind or rabbits or bugs or the strongest strains of weeds. Yet most of us don't let these things keep us from planting.

With this same sort of faith we can tend to ourselves. Though we don't know what each day will bring, we can plant the seeds in ourselves to meet most anything. We can rise each morning determined to give what we have. We can't plant the seeds for others, and we can't keep the storms from coming. The beauty is, we don't have to.

What seeds of joy can I plant today?

April 20

> *Hurried and worried until we're buried*
> *And there's no curtain call,*
> *Life's a very funny proposition,*
>   *after all.*
>
> —George M. Cohan

Often, when we involve ourselves in a whirl-wind of activities, plans, and expectations, we push ourselves so hard that we don't derive any satisfaction from success. We need to face our limitations. We can't do everything we want. Even when we can do a great deal, if we overextend ourselves, take on too much, we will not enjoy ourselves, and there is no reason not to enjoy our work.

Our activities are part of what we are. If we choose to live in a frantic hurry, worrying about the next moment instead of this one, we'll miss life entirely. Part of self-knowledge is learning to pace ourselves to our own speed, learning to set goals we can attain for each day. When we do this, we can say, "Now that I've completed this, I don't have to do one more thing to feel worthwhile."

Am I trying to do too much too fast?

*In grief, healing helps us make peace
with the meaning of death, which cannot be understood except as an unknown part of life.*
        —Alla Bozarth-Campbell

It is a sad occasion when we must say goodbye
to a loved one or pet who has died. But grief is the
only way we can come to understand our losses,
and sharing grief helps us experience it more fully.

Perhaps we wish to grieve for something else
we've lost, like fading youth, a job, a possession,
or a habit we had come to enjoy. It's natural to feel
grief over things like this, too.

We can share stories and good memories with
other grievers, and give free reign to our tears.
Sometimes it seems the more we talk, the sadder
we feel about our losses, but when we share these
feelings with others, we turn our losses into gain.
We heal ourselves, pay tribute to those we grieve
for, and share an intimate sense of loss with someone else.

Do I have grief to share?

April 22

I meant to do my work today
But a brown bird sang in an apple tree,
And a butterfly flitted across the field
And all the leaves were calling me.
              —Richard LeGallienne

The harried hen scurried about her house, trying to put it in order. Some friends she hadn't seen for years were due to arrive later that day, and she wanted everything perfect for them. In a flurry, she made the bed, put away the dishes, and scrubbed the floor. Oh dear, she thought in dismay, I meant to wash the sheets today. Frantically, she flew back to the bedroom and tore the sheets from the made bed.

Just then, a neighbor arrived and stood at hen's door, watching her anxiously rush about. "Dear hen," he said in a patient loving tone, for he was quite fond of her, "You will never enjoy your visit if you continue to race about. Come. Sit and rest and tell me of these friends. Have you any snapshots?" The hen did as her neighbor had suggested, and soon her friends arrived to find her relaxed, refreshed, and warm with the memories of them.

What is my real work for the day?

*Courage is resistance to fear, mastery of
fear not absence of fear.*
                                    —*Mark Twain*

It is not unusual to feel afraid. It is unusual,
however, to hear anyone admit to feeling afraid.
Sometimes we think there are some people who
are so cool and calm that they never feel afraid.
This may make us think we're not as good because
we know how often we feel afraid. This is why it is
important to think about what courage really is. It
is not the absence of fear. Courage is not letting
fear stop us from doing what we need to do.

We might have to get up in front of a group to
give a speech. We could give in to our fear and not
give the speech, or we could admit our fear to
those who love us, and then go ahead and do the
best we can. To go ahead in the face of fear is
courage.

What am I afraid of?

April 24

My life has been a tapestry of rich and
* royal hue,*
An everlasting vision of the everchang-
* ing view,*
A wondrous woven magic in bits of
* blue and gold,*
A tapestry to feel and see, impossible to
* hold.*

—Carole King

Our lives are patchwork quilts of mismatched fabrics, all stitched together by an invisible seamstress. The tattered, blood-red scraps of quarrels, the beige of pastry crust baked on Saturdays in a grandmother's kitchen that always smelled sweet, the brilliant colors of our happy moments — picnics and sunsets and laughter — all these are necessary pieces of the tapestry of our lives, even our cold, white doubts and emptiness.

All the colors of life sewn together with the green thread of growth. We are a mixture of feelings and experiences. Often, we want to cut away a square of painful memory. But without it, our quilt would lose its beauty, for contrast would disappear. If a piece is removed, the rest is weakened and incomplete.

How well can I accept any pain I feel today as a part of my own beauty?

Unused capacities atrophy, cease to be.
—Tillie Olsen

Those of us who have suffered a broken bone and had to put up with a cast for several weeks know how hard it is to use muscles that have been inactive for so long. They have gotten weak from lack of use, and we have to begin to develop our strength all over again.

The same thing happens if we don't use our other capacities. If we don't constantly use our minds to think and learn, we become dull people, almost incapable of new thoughts and insights. If we don't use our hearts to love, we become uncaring and insensitive — much like Scrooge in *A Christmas Carol.* If we don't use our creative talents — to draw or write or sew, or whatever it is we're into — we lose the ability to do those things.

On the other hand, like our muscles, our other capacities can be strengthened and developed by daily use. We exercise our hearts by being kind and loving, our minds by thinking, our imaginations by being creative. In this way, we become spiritually powerful, a force for good in the world.

How can I exercise my assets today?

April 26

> "The horror of that moment," the King
> went on, "I shall never forget."
> "You will, though," the Queen said, "if
> you don't make a memorandum of it."
> —Lewis Carroll

Crises come in many forms. When we are in the middle of any kind of crisis, we may feel like we have fallen into a deep hole. We may see no way out, and begin to feel hopeless and overwhelmed by the size and darkness of the hole.

Yet we are not alone. An animal caught in a hole would cry out until someone came along and helped it out. We, too, can call out for help — to our Higher Power and to the important people in our lives. We can learn to trust that, with the help of our friends and our Higher Power, we will be able to crawl out of our holes.

With trust, we will climb out of our crises and be healed with the passage of time. Such holes are a part of our landscape, yet every time, we will be able to climb out and walk, leaving the darkness behind us.

What help can I ask for today?

Crying only a little bit is no use.
You must cry until your pillow
   is soaked.
Then you can get up and laugh. . . .
                    —Galway Kinnell

Many of us were raised to deny our feelings; that is, we might have been allowed to describe them politely, but we were not allowed to express feelings on the spot by wailing, jumping for joy, or dancing. This is often considered rude. In a proper home, we often hear, if people have feelings, they have them quietly. But many of us have suffered living this way.

We need a full and thorough expression of a feeling in order to know it, experience it, and move beyond it. This is the way we let go of sadness, for instance.

Feelings come and go. If we are not afraid to let them have their moment, we will not be afraid to express them.

What am I feeling right now?

April 28

I will not cut my conscience to fit this year's fashions.

—Lillian Hellman

Every fall there seems to be something new and different to get for school — a special folder, a new style of pants, or maybe a different haircut. These things change from year to year.

Sometimes we get carried away with the current trends. We start putting too much importance on such things. We may be tempted to join our friends in teasing someone who doesn't wear the "right" clothes, or avoid someone who doesn't say the "right" things. This is when we need God's help. Perhaps we can become the leaders for the next trend — looking beyond appearances of others to the beauty inside them.

Will I see the true value in those around me today?

If there is a God, there must also be a Goddess. Neither is more important than the other, both are in balance, together they create a Whole.
—Marion Weinstein

In the olden days, the Goddess was seen as a Trinity: the Maiden or Virgin, the Mother, and the Crone. The Virgin was one-in-herself, owned by no man. The Mother was the one in the fullness of her creative powers, whether creating children, works of art, or other work out in the world. The Crone was the wise old woman.

Both women and men connected with the Triple Goddess. To women, the Goddess was a symbol of their innermost selves and the beneficent, nurturing, liberating power within. The Crone, for example, showed them that all phases of life are sacred, that age is a blessing rather than a curse. To men, the Goddess represented their connection with their own hidden female selves.

We are all made up of aspects of both sexes. This is our balance. When we accept what we know to be truly ourselves, which is often much more than the old role models for men and women allow, we become complete men and women.

What male and female strengths do I have within me?

April 30

> *The soul would have no rainbow had*
> *the eyes no tears.*
> —*John Vance Cheney*

If there were no rain, fields would become parched and brittle, and many creatures would die. If we could not cry, all our emotions would eventually dry up, too, and soon we would not laugh either. Our tears cleanse us. Our tears heal. They make us whole.

Tears are as important to our growth as rain is to a flower. They help release the pressure of sadness so we can feel better. After a storm, when the sun shines again through the clouds, a brightly colored rainbow appears. After our tears, our inner sun shines, and rainbows are formed from our pain.

How well can I accept my tears as part of my happiness today?

May

Hold fast to dreams
For if dreams die,
Life is a broken-winged bird
That cannot fly.
                            —Langston Hughes

Watching birds spread their wings and soar can remind us of the best in ourselves. In joyful moments we all feel our own desire to fly, to reach toward what we dream of doing.

Our dreams give us a direction to fly. Birds fly toward the light for joy, toward green leaves for shelter, to water and berries for food. In the same way, our dreams direct us to the source of our own joy, shelter, and nourishment.

Sometimes as we fly, we bump into disappointments. They may temporarily stun us or slow us down. But just like birds that are occasionally wounded, we can heal ourselves and fly again. We can choose to not let the hardships of life break our spirited wings. Rather, we can keep spreading our wings, soaring in the spirit of joy.

Am I flying today, or must I heal a wound first?

> *A bird came down the walk:*
> *He did not know I saw;*
> *He bit an angle-worm in halves*
> *And ate the fellow, raw.*
> —*Emily Dickinson*

We must look very different to the birds than we do to each other. Likewise, birds seem different to us than they do to each other. Neither the way we see birds or the way they see us is the "right" way. They are simply different ways of seeing.

If we could turn birds into people so they would see things the way we do, eat the way we do, and think the way we do, we would lose the idea of flying. The knowledge that flight is possible is a gift birds have given us.

We do well to remember this when we get upset at others for not doing things the way we would. Variety of styles, appetites, and ideas is a gift that enriches the world and brings more possibilities into our lives.

When others disagree with me today, will I accept their gift?

*Everyone has talent. What is rare is the
courage to follow the talent.*
                              —*Erica Jong*

How easy it is to look at others with envy, certain that everyone we know is better in every way: school, sports, games, appearance. What we may not know is that each of us is exactly right the way we are. And what's more, no one of us is without talent. Perhaps we simply have not discovered it yet, or maybe we've been certain we knew what the talent should be, rather than letting the talent within us emerge.

It's reassuring to know that we are talented, that we are special just as we are, that no one else is able to bring to this life exactly the same ingredients that we're able to bring.

What special talent shall I exercise today?

May 4

*A person can grow only as much as his
horizon allows.*
                              —*John Powell*

Should you be a doctor or perhaps an astro-
naut? Maybe being a writer or an athlete appeals
to you. Dreaming of what to be can be useful. It
helps us set our goals and learn our values. Also,
using our imagination lets us "try on" a future role.
We learn about our life's direction through our
dreams of where to go and what to do.

Not all dreams are helpful, however. Sometimes
we daydream about other things when we really
do need to listen. Learning how to use our imagination to guide our plans for growing up takes
practice.

Imagining ourselves happy and brave will help
us feel both. Imagining ourselves as failures can be
just as powerful. Let's respect the power of the
imagination and use it to form good images of our
future.

*How can I build goodness and success into my
future today?*

*I have spread my dreams under
 your feet;
Tread softly because you tread on
 my dreams.*
                    —*William Butler Yeats*

When we hold a piece of crystal to the light, it paints rainbows on the wall. When we tap it lightly with a spoon, it sings like a bell. But when we drop it, it shatters in colorless, silent pieces on the floor.

Human beings, sometimes to our amazement, can be as fragile as glass. Especially with people we live with or have known for a long time, it's easy to forget what makes them shine or sing. We take for granted the very qualities that made us love them in the first place.

When we forget how to see and hear the people we love, how to appreciate them, we grow careless. Too often, from sheer neglect, the relationship between us grows dull and silent, then slips, falls, and shatters. Paying attention to other people's needs and feelings can prevent this.

Whose presence can I appreciate today?

May 6

> *"Take it away at once,"* stormed the
> *Princess, stamping her tiny foot in its*
> *embroidered slipper. "I hate real*
> *flowers; their petals fall off and they*
> *die."*
>
> —*Hans Christian Andersen*

If love is reserved for things that never die, love
is doomed to die. If flowers fade in a minute or
two, will not stones wear to sand in time? Even this
earth, this garden of life, one day will be like the
dust of stars. We must walk gratefully, carefully on
it now. Now is the lifetime that passes here, now is
the best of all days; now is the flower's eternity in
the sun, our chance of a lifetime.

This is all we have, this moment. Within it, anything can be done, any dream fulfilled, if we only
use it well. Why hold back? There is nothing to
stop us.

What can I do to use this moment well?

*Our deeds still travel with us from afar,
and what we have been makes us what
we are.*

—George Eliot

We grow within the way a tree does. We've all seen the rings representing the years of a tree's life. We carry our histories with us, too. Our actions, our attitudes, our goals, and our dreams all gather together inside us to make us what we are today. We're probably ashamed of some of our past, but our behavior each day adds to our history, and we control it.

We can't escape our past mistakes, but we don't have to repeat them; and every day that is lived well gives us a history to be proud of.

How can I add goodness to my past — and my future — by my actions today?

May 8

Talking little, and
with the low, tender part
of our voices, as in nodding to one
    who already
knows what you mean.
                    —*Tess Gallagher*

Once there was a small child whose only word
was *no*. When she wanted to indicate yes, she nod-
ded her head emphatically. What she liked to do
instead of talk was play. She liked to play outside
in the meadow with the bugs and rocks and plants.

The mullein was her favorite plant. She rubbed
the soft, furry leaves across her cheek. Her mother
told her that, in the old days, American Indians
used these leaves as bandages. Several years later,
Lucy picked a mullein leaf and took it in the house
to her mother. "Look, Mama. Indian owee."

We, too, can remember some surprising things
from the dim past, before we could talk or understand all that went on around us. Communication
does not always depend on words alone but on the
tenderness with which they are spoken. Walking
through the world in a tender, loving way is a form
of communication that goes beyond words to our
deepest feelings.

What are some of the ways we show our love
without words?

Planning is deciding what to change to-day so tomorrow will be different from yesterday.

—Ichak Adizes

A house is like a lump of clay that can be molded and changed. It can be fixed and shaped, torn down and added to, painted, papered, carpeted, and panelled. We can think about how to change it, find pictures in books, and order plans. We can stock up on supplies, take fix-it classes, and get advice from others. But the house will remain unchanged until we pick up a brush, grab a bucket of paint, and get to work. Only then will we see tomorrow the results of what we did today.

Our plans help us construct a vision of how we'd like the future to be, but only actions will bring these things about. With confidence in the rightness of our desires, we can be assured that God never gives us a dream we can't reach.

What action can I take today to make tomorrow's changes?

May 10

> *To apologize: to lay the foundation for*
> *a future offense.*
> > —*Ambrose Bierce*

"I'm sorry," said the blind man as he whipped the mare. "I'm sorry," said the mare, as she kicked the blind man in return.

"We're sorry," they assured themselves, as they pushed each other around again and again. Often, we push our troubles with other people around, creeping along in the old, rough way, refusing to change because we're too involved to see another choice.

There's little sorrow in being sorry all the time. A true apology doesn't try to explain. Sometimes a true apology just breaks down and cries. Then maybe we're ready to go on — take someone by the hand, tell the whole sad truth, and work to find a better way.

Are my apologies excuses, or requests to be forgiven?

I'm delighted that the future is unsure.
That's the way it should be.
　　　　—William Sloane Coffin

Some of life's richest moments are the most unexpected: the old friend met by chance, or the new one discovered when neither of us were really looking; the toy at the bottom of the toy box, rediscovered and loved anew; the book, the flower, the shaft of light we were in the right place at the right time to notice and embrace.

It is important to dream and plan, to work toward goals, to mark the milestones we pass on life's journey. No less important, though, is to open ourselves to the unexpected joys awaiting us every day.

Am I ready, today, to expect the unexpected?

May 12

I would be honest, for there are those who trust me.
—Howard Arnold Walter

Some of those around us seem to see only the good in us. They trust and respect us, even when we ourselves may not feel we deserve it.

A young girl once talked about her grandfather. She said, "He was the only person in my life who saw the good in me." She mentioned that she sought to please her grandfather and not disappoint the trust which he placed in her. He brought out the best in her because of the way that he looked at her. Each of us can be like this grandfather by focusing on the good in other people. We can use our spiritual eyes to see love, honesty, trustworthiness, and unselfishness in the heart of another. As we look for the good, we are doing our part to help create it.

Do I see the good in those around me right now?

*Talent — I don't know what that is. It's
will. You dream a dream and then you
build it.*

—Philippe Petit

Even the most accomplished pianists begin at
some point by playing simple scales and exercises.
With daily practice, their hands learn to find the
correct notes and become limber enough to play
well. They learn each new piece of music very
slowly at first, until, with study and practice, they
can play almost without effort.

In the beginning, the pianist only dreams of being an accomplished musician. This dream helps
the artist through many hours of practice and
study.

Talent is really the combination of a dream and
the time spent building it. We develop our ability
by devoting time to the skills that interest us. Like
the musician, we become talented through daily
practice — the daily building of a dream. By developing our talents, we develop who we are.

Who am I becoming today?

May 14

Every tomorrow has two handles. We can take hold of it with the handle of anxiety or the handle of faith.
—Henry Ward Beecher

Once there was a boy who always looked on the bright side and always expected the best. He expected to like brussels sprouts before he had ever tasted them, for instance, and to like his teacher on the first day of school. Because he had such a sunny outlook on things, he was rarely disappointed.

But the boy's father thought he wasn't realistic, so one Christmas he decided to test him. On Christmas morning there were many presents, all but one small one were for the boy's brother. The brother opened his gifts with glee — a train set, a toy robot, a cowboy outfit, even his own TV.

Through all this, the boy smiled expectantly, confident the contents of his small box would equal the splendor of his brother's gifts. When it was his turn he ripped the box open to find only a pile of hay and some very smelly animal droppings.

To his father's astonishment, the boy clapped his hands with joy and ran immediately to the backyard. "Yippee!" he cried. "There must be a pony here somewhere!"

If I expect the best, just for today, what wondrous things might happen?

What is moral is what you feel good after.

—*Ernest Hemingway*

Each of us has a little voice inside us that tells us what is good and what is bad. For instance, if our friends are making fun of someone who is different than we are, how do we feel if we join in the laughter? Do we feel more comfortable if we refuse to join in, or if we tell them their jokes are not funny?

As we grow, we learn more and more to trust the inner voice. Sometimes, in times of dark confusion, we have to listen very hard, but it is there to guide us. It is a beacon showing us the way out of the darkness of uncertainty. It is our guide to goodness.

Will I have the courage to listen to my inner voice today?

May 16

More majestic than a cardinal, as shin-
ing as a pyx.
—*Gustave Flaubert*

What in the world is a pyx? If we don't have an expert nearby, we'll have to look in a book. There we'll find it defined, explained, fixed. Now what in the world is love? It doesn't live in a tree or a book, so where in the world do we look? Can we find love in the house, maybe swept under the rug? Can we know the feel of it in our hands, see it written on the lines of faces we know? Does it make a sound — maybe laugh and cry? Does it know how to speak, form words carefully, write letters? Is it only written on the heart?

We find love inside us, and our love seeks itself out in others. We find it in the familiar footfall of a brother or sister, the sound of a parent's voice in the next room, and yet, too often we don't express it directly. When we do, our love thrives in all we do together.

What does love have to do with the ordinary facts of life?

Growth is the only evidence of life.
—John, Cardinal Newman

We should be thankful we can never reach complete serenity. If we could, we would never have the need to improve ourselves. We would stop growing, because there would be no reason to learn any more than we already know, and we would become bored. Even the things which seem so serene in nature usually contain a struggle within. A lake, with a swan gliding slowly across it, seems a perfect picture of serenity. But, unseen below the surface, fish, turtles, and frogs struggle each day for survival.

The important thing is to accept the struggles as a part of the beauty of life, not as blemishes on it.

What struggles shall help me grow better today?

May 18

He that cannot forgive others breaks the bridge over which he must pass himself; for every man has need to be forgiven.

—Thomas Fuller

We have all seen adventure movies in which the heroes or villains are caught on a bridge that collapses. As they fall to whatever lies below, they are perhaps able to climb to one side or the other. But for the time being, their ability to cross between the two sides is gone.

When we have been hurt by people in our lives, or when we have hurt others, mutual forgiveness is needed in order to rebuild the trust between us. It is very much like rebuilding a bridge — one piece at a time. We take cautious steps at first — testing the safety and strength of our bridge.

When two people have become separated by loss or anger, it is forgiveness that can rebuild the bridge between them. Forgiveness needs time and so does the rebuilding of trust.

Can I begin to rebuild a friendship today?

As we learn we always change, and so our perception. This changed perception then becomes a new Teacher inside each of us.

—Hyemeyohsts Storm

Hyemeyohsts Storm's book, *Seven Arrows*, tells the stories of one of the Indian tribes in this country before most its members were killed. They believed that change was important for growth. Change is sometimes frightening. We usually prefer the familiar, no matter how uncomfortable, over taking a chance on the unknown.

When fear gets in the way of making healthy changes, we talk to fear, inviting it along with us on our course of action. Getting to know fear allows us to ask it for a gift: the courage to walk with fear by our side and learn from it as we go. It allows us to learn which fear is blocking our progress and which fear is healthy — cautioning us against actions that might be harmful.

What fear might I make a friend of today?

May 20

> *For nothing can be sole or whole that*
> *has not been rent.*
> — *W. B. Yeats*

The maple out front is young and healthy, but it grows in the shape of a Y. Neighborhood tree experts have warned that, as it grows, it will split in half as the weight of the two main branches pull down against each other. One of those two beautiful branches, already lush with new leaves, must be cut. But once pruned, the remaining branch will straighten as it reaches for the sun. It will grow faster, and the whole tree will live many years longer — all by cutting it back today.

Sometimes we are like this tree. We go in too many directions, and can't seem to do any one thing well. When this happens, we need to give something up, to choose which direction we want and stick with it. The results will be well worth the price.

What is holding me back from growth?

*Who will tell whether one happy mo-
ment of love or the joy of breathing or
walking on a bright morning and
smelling the fresh air, is not worth all
the suffering and effort which life implies. . . .*

—Erich Fromm

A robin comes alive by breaking out of its shell.
The small bird struggles to break out of the safety
of the blue egg. Once out, it struggles to grow,
slowly learning how to eat, walk, and fly.

We, too, struggle as we grow. There is broken-
ness in all of our lives — broken hearts and broken
dreams. Yet these experiences open our way to a
world of growing. We find comfort in the presence
of a Power greater than ourselves, in the same way
a baby bird finds warmth near the body of its
mother. We, too, can grow stronger every day,
learning to take in nourishment and trying out our
new wings.

*What struggles have made me as strong as I am
today?*

May 22

If it's sanity you're after, there's no rec-
ipe like laughter.
—Henry Rutherford Elliot

A smile is the earliest form of communication. A human infant smiles in the first few weeks of life. As the child grows, it learns how to turn the smile into a laugh — a joyous response reflecting pleasure.

A sense of humor, a feeling of fun, and an ability to laugh are all signs of emotional maturity. Healthy laughter frees us; it is the sunshine that makes life's shadows interesting. When we develop the ability to see the humor in a situation, we gain the ability to handle it.

We were born with smiles. They are as much a part of us as our teeth and hair. Polished and cared for, our smiles can grow into a sense of humor that will help us through the painful times.

How can I turn troubles into smiles today?

*The prayer of the chicken hawk does
not get him the chicken.*
                    —Swahili proverb

Imagine flying high over the grassy plains
searching with piercing eyes for dinner down below. The sun is warm on our backs as we catch the
heated updrafts and rest, always watching, always
praying, that dinner will be provided for the little
ones back in the nest.

Dinner will be provided, of that the hawk is
sure. It has faith. But the faith and the prayer will
not put the chicken in its talons. It is going to have
to keep looking, and, when it spots the prey, its
wings will fold back, and its sleek body will plum-
met out of the sky. It will brake quickly with broad
wings and clasp the unsuspecting supper on the
fly.

Like the hawk, once we have prayed, we must
get to work. Our goal isn't going to be done for us.
We can pray for the strength and wisdom we will
need to get it done, and that prayer will be answered. But, as the hawk knows, it's up to us to do
the work.

*What is my goal today, and my first step toward
it?*

May 24

Spring does not ask an audience, but shapes each blossom perfectly, indifferent to applause.
—*Joan Walsh Anglund*

In the spring each blossom brings its own shape, color, and fragrance. The lilacs come early to spread their lavender splash. Apple trees burst into white, cherry blossoms into pink, and each weaves its unique and pleasant perfume.

They don't bloom because someone told them to, or because they will receive anything in return. They bloom for the pure joy of blooming. They bloom because that is what they are here to do.

Each one of us blooms in our own time, with our own color and fragrance. Every one of us is a special and important blossom, and we are all part of the tree of life.

How will my day today help me grow?

*Do we really know anybody? Who
does not wear one face to hide another?*
—Francis Marion

A woman in her fifties watched her mother in
her eighties struggle against the wrinkles in her
face and neck, trying to hide them, to pretend they
weren't there. She wanted her mother to accept
that she was getting older but found her unwilling
to listen.

Haven't we all run into this situation? We can
learn so much just by remembering that what is
right for one person may not be right for another,
and others are entitled to decide how they want to
behave. Often, we are just worried about ourselves, concerned, for instance, with our own ability to age gracefully. We don't need someone else to
do it for us. We can take care of that ourselves.

*What do I worry about in another that I can take
care of in myself?*

May 26

> *An oak and a reed were arguing about*
> *their strength. When a strong wind*
> *came up, the reed avoided being up-*
> *rooted by bending and leaning with the*
> *gusts of wind. But the oak stood firm*
> *and was torn up by the roots.*
>
> — *Aesop*

Within each of us, as in the reed and the oak, is
a single characteristic which is both our strongest
and weakest trait. The bending which keeps the
reed alive makes it weak, we might think. Some of
us see both sides of every argument and are good
team players, fair judges, and compassionate
friends. But like the reed — always bending to the
needs of others — we may never know what we
want or who we are.

Some of us believe we are like the oak: strong
and tough and successful in the face of most difficulty. But we may never learn to accept flaws in
ourselves.

We are wise to remember that no trait is strong
or weak, but we make it so by how we use it. We
can use our strength to stand straight in the face of
hardship, and we can use our strength to bend.

What is my strongest and weakest trait?

*If your life is ever going to get better,
you'll have to take risks. There is simply no way you can grow without taking chances.*

—David Viscott

One sunny day a caterpillar who was afraid of
the dark came to a tunnel which lay squarely in its
path. It had a choice of going back where it
started, or summoning the courage to crawl into
the darkness. "What shall I do?" wondered the
caterpillar. "If I go back home, I won't get where I
want to go, but I'm so afraid!"

Just then, a voice called out from the tunnel. "I
can hear you, Mr. Caterpillar. I am Mr. Beetle. I
am here in the tunnel and I can see the other end. If
you come through, you won't lose your fear of the
dark, but you will get where you want to go."

We are all like the caterpillar once in a while.
But if we let our fear stop us from doing things
which are necessary to our growth, we will never
realize what courage we really have.

Is my fear a necessary part of new experiences?

May 28

Though we travel the world over to find the beautiful, we must carry it with us or we find it not.
—Ralph Waldo Emerson

The little rabbit stood alone, watching her family and friends hop and skip about her in the forest, playing her favorite rabbit game. Try as she might, each time she attempted to join in, she tripped about awkwardly. When this happened, the other rabbits laughed uproariously at her and called her "Grace." Soon even she forgot her real name. But in the moments when Grace was alone, she danced around the trees with ease. She was as smooth and graceful as any ballerina. An old owl sat high above her one night, watching her intently. The moonlight streamed through the treetops like a soft spotlight and he sat and watched as little Grace move in and out of the moonbeams. Finally he said, "Grace, you are more graceful than any creature I've ever seen." Grace was startled that someone had been watching her, but listened carefully to the wise owl's words as he continued. "You have carried this beauty within you all the time, but locked it inside when you tried too hard." If we remember to relax and trust in ourselves, we, too, will discover that we are able.

What hidden ability can I set loose today?

The only people who never fail are those who never try.
　　　　　　　　　　—Ilka Chase

A boy once asked his grandfather how he had become so happy and successful in his life. "Right decisions," replied his grandfather. The boy thought for a while and then asked a second question, "But how do you learn to make right decisions?" The grandfather answered quickly with a twinkle in his eye, "Wrong decisions!"

We, too, will learn from our "wrong decisions," our mistakes. Whenever we try anything, there is always the possibility of failure. We must learn to not let this keep us from trying. When we are willing to try, we have already conquered our fear. We can grow no matter what the outcome is.

What failure have I turned into success?

May 30

The cut worm forgives the plow.
—William Blake

Would anyone believe that rain abuses grass, or accuse roots, hungry for a better hold on life, of digging too far into earth's flesh? And if the earth should have to quake, would anyone blame it for cracking here and there? Look closely at the small world of busy life overturned in the garden each spring. No ant there curses another bug, and no worm curses itself. Though they can neither speak nor think, even small creatures know enough to accept their pain as a natural part of life.

Why, then, should we waste time blaming others, or ourselves, for the natural sensations of life?

In the process of new growth, can we expect no pain?

> *It is only with the heart that one can*
> *see rightly; what is essential is invisible*
> *to the eye.*
> —*Antoine de St. Exupery*

A tuning fork is a small tool that is used to tune musical instruments. It is tapped softly and then set down. As it vibrates, it gives off a musical tone. When its vibrations perfectly match the vibrations of the note played on the instrument, the instrument is in tune. When the note matches the tuning fork, this can be both felt and heard.

Our hearts work like a tuning fork. When the heart feels completely in tune with a decision or thought or action in our lives, then we know it is the right one for us. We can actually feel the harmony inside our bodies.

Sometimes what we know deep in our hearts gets clouded over by doubts and questions and other people's opinions and judgments. We need to clear away such clouds and listen to our hearts, for our hearts carry the wisdom of God.

Am I in tune with my heart today?

June

*Everything has its wonders, even dark-
ness and silence, and I learn whatever
state I may be in, therein to be content.*
          —Helen Keller

Close observation of small children playing,
ants moving across a dirt mound, a bird building a
nest, a plane flying overhead, tomatoes ripening in
a garden are quiet reminders of the many miracles
surrounding us at any moment. Often we may
wonder just how a carrot grows from a small seed.
What enables a robin to fly south in the winter
without getting lost? And then we remember the
power of the Creator, and the presence of that
power everywhere.

Just as the squirrel knows to collect nuts for
winter, each of us knows we're always being
watched over by God. When we remember that,
we feel safe and happy wherever we are, at school,
a new friend's house, home alone in the evening.
Every moment is full of wonder, and God is always present.

What small things will I share with God today?

June 2

*Thoughts, rest your wings. Here is a
hollow of silence, a nest of stillness, in
which to hatch your dreams.*
—*Joan Walsh Anglund*

There is silence in the nest before an egg is
hatched. The mother robin must sit quietly and
warm them enough to be hatched. During this
time, the mother concentrates only on her eggs.
She does not let herself be distracted.

There is a time of silence before anything creative is born. And there is silence in the mind before
an idea is discovered. A nest is a safe place birds
can always return to and be at home. We all need
such a nest of silence — a place where we can be
quiet and safe, where we can let ourselves be held,
and rest.

Often, our best ideas come out of these quiet
moments. Times of silence are good for our souls.
Just like the robin eggs hatching, so will dreams
and solutions grow out of our own nest of stillness.

How well will I use my quiet time today?

*Men will find that they can prepare
with mutual aid far more easily what
they need and avoid far more easily the
perils which beset them on all sides, by
united forces.*

—*Baruch Spinoza*

Three travellers stopped in a small town on their
way to the city. They had tents to sleep in, but no
food or money. They knocked on doors asking for
a little food, but the people were poor, with little
to eat and nothing to spare.

Cheerfully, they returned to their camp and
built a fire. "What are you doing?" asked a bystander, "Building a fire with nothing to cook?"

"But we do have something to cook!" they said.
"Our favorite dish, stone soup. We only need a
pot."

"I think I can find one," said one of the by-
standers, And she ran home to fetch it.

When she returned, the travellers filled the pot
with water and placed two large stones in it. "This
will be the finest soup we've ever made!" said the
first traveller. "I agree," said the second, "but don't
you think it would taste better with a cabbage in
it?"

"I think I can find one," said another bystander.

And so it went the whole afternoon until, by
evening, the travellers had a hearty, fragrant feast,
which they shared with the hungry townspeople.

*What can I do with help today, that I couldn't do
alone?*

June 4

> *"Oh, 'tis love, 'tis love, that makes the world go round! Somebody said," Alice whispered, "that it's done by everybody minding their own business. Ah well! It means much the same thing."*
> —Lewis Carroll

No one helps a caterpillar become a butterfly. First it must crawl through the leaves as a many-legged creature, and then it weaves its own cocoon. Nature does its slow, daily work inside the cocoon and one day a butterfly emerges — and each butterfly is a different shape and color. No other creature can step in and speed up this process without hurting the butterfly.

Sometimes we humans confuse love with playing the part of God. We think we can speed up the natural growth of people around us. We interfere by telling them to do what we think best.

Sometimes the greatest love we can offer is to accept our loved ones the way they are. We need to remember that each caterpillar weaves a cocoon in its own time and becomes a butterfly in its own way. The wisdom of the universe is greater than our own.

How will I show my acceptance of others today?

*To render ourselves insensible to pain
we must forfeit also the possibilities of
happiness.*
                        —*Sir John Lubbock*

A caterpillar knows instinctively that it must
spin a cocoon. When finished it will use the protection it has made to turn itself into a beautiful butterfly. When the time is right, the butterfly will
break through the cocoon and stretch its wings to
meet the world.

We sometimes protect ourselves by withdrawing
into a cocoon of our own. We stop talking to others and find ourselves growing lonely and longing
for our friends. Perhaps it was some pain that
made us retreat, but the pain of loneliness is
greater. When we have the courage to break out of
our cocoon, knowing and accepting the fact that
we will experience both pain and happiness, we
will change. We will become, for that moment,
something new and beautiful like the butterfly.

*What fearful thing do I have the courage to face
today?*

June 6

A good anger acted upon is beautiful as lightning and swift with power. A good anger swallowed clots the blood like slime.

—Marge Piercy

How does it feel when someone tells us we should play basketball when we don't want to? Often, it angers us that someone else is telling us what to do. After we have been told we should do something many times, we begin to believe it and forget how we really feel. Even though we have forgotten what we wanted to do, we feel angry, often without realizing it. Such hidden anger can leave us feeling bad without knowing why.

It is important to know when we are angry, and to say so. There are healthy ways of expressing anger without blaming others. Saying we are angry, and thereby claiming it as our own feeling and not something others force on us, is a way to express it which also affirms our right to be angry.

If there is anger in me today, can I express it correctly?

*The human brain forgets ninety percent
of what goes on.*
                                    —*Jan Milner*

There were two women who shared a house and
raised their daughters, two toddlers, together.
Then one of the women got transferred to another
city and moved with her daughter.

Ten years later, they had a reunion. The mothers
asked their kids what they remembered about living together. Did they remember all the books?
No. Did they remember a mom in the kitchen
every morning, fixing eggs and toast? No.

What they remembered was playing in the pink
bathtub for hours, pulling the pink shower curtain
shut for privacy. And the morning the mothers
sneaked in, turned off the lights, threw plastic cups
and spoons over the curtain and cried, "It's raining
spoons!" They laughed and laughed.

We are lucky in this life — our minds think
laughter is what's worth remembering.

*What laughter from yesterday can I remember to-
day?*

June 8

*Caring is everything; nothing matters
but caring.*
    —Baron Friedrich Von Hugel

The caring we receive from someone we love
when we're sick can heal us just as much as the
medicine we take. For children, Mom is usually the
one who makes sure we get enough rest by having
us stay in bed. By bringing us juice and aspirins
she helps us keep our fevers down. She also lifts
our spirits when she tells us a funny story.

Perhaps the next time a loved one is sick we can
do the special and caring things. We can bring a
favorite magazine or a cold glass of water, tell a
joke, or just sit and be there for a while. Whether
the sick person is a parent or a brother or sister,
when we help care for another, we complete a circle of caring begun by a parent so long ago.

Does someone need my care today?

We never know how high we are
'Til we are called to rise;
And then, if we are true to plan,
Our statures touch the skies.
　　　　　—Emily Dickinson

We are all capable of far more than we think we are. It's in the tough times, however, that we discover the depths of our strength, and it's then that we know that some power has enabled us to do what we thought we could not. Whatever we call that power, it is there for us when we need it.

To do what seems impossible, all we need to do is ask for the help we think we need. And we can look within, too, and summon our whole selves to the task at hand. With all that going for us, how can we fail? And when the tough work is over, we'll look back and know we've grown from the experience. And yes, our statures will have touched the skies.

When I am faced with a tough task, how do I respond?

June 10

Whoever I am or whatever I am doing, some kind of excellence is within my reach.
— John W. Gardner

It's easy to forget how important we each are — to our parents, to other family members, to our friends. We are in this world, even in our particular family, because we are important and necessary in the lives of others. It's easy to feel not so important though, especially when we think we're not good enough at anything we try. School or work comes easy for some. Maybe not us. Athletics come easy to others. Maybe it's helping around the house that's easiest. Each of us is very good at some things. And it's okay to not be good at everything.

How can I show my talent today?

Worry never robs tomorrow of its sorrow, but only saps today of its strength.

—*A. J. Cronin*

There is always something to worry about. What if it rains tomorrow on the family picnic? What if the baby gets sick and we can't go? What if we can't find a shady spot for our lunch table? Will the water be too cold for swimming? Will the boat motor conk out in the middle of the lake? What if we forget the charcoal? Or the lighter fluid?

Today, while preparing the potato salad for tomorrow's picnic, all we need to know is whether the potatoes are cool enough to peel and slice.

Our worries about tomorrow change nothing but ourselves, and they have nothing to do with what we are doing right now. Tomorrow will become today soon enough, and today is the day we have.

Which of my worries belong only to tomorrow, and should be left alone until then?

June 12

> *The more a diamond is cut the more it*
> *sparkles.*
>
> —*Anonymous*

There is something of value to be found even in the worst of things. Consider the oyster. When a grain of sand penetrates an oyster's shell, it irritates the oyster, making it uncomfortable. The oyster relieves the pain by coating the sand with a soothing liquid. When this liquid hardens, a pearl is formed. The very process that healed the oyster created a precious jewel for others to cherish and admire.

The way in which we deal with our own frustrations — painful though they may be — can make a difference. Pearls can be formed from our experiences, making us wiser and stronger, or grains of sand — anger, bitterness, resentment — can remain imbedded inside us. The choice is ours.

How can I turn my irritations into pearls today?

Let the gentle bush dig its root deep and
spread upward to split one boulder.
                                        —Carl Sandburg

There is a fable about the sun and wind having a contest to see who can get the old man to take his coat off first. The wind blows fiercely, but the old man just pulls his coat tighter around him. Finally, the wind gives up and the sun comes out. The sun shines a steady warm light down on the old man, who soon takes his coat off.

More and better things are accomplished in this world by kindness and gentleness than by force. When we find ourselves most frustrated, it is often because we are trying to force certain things to happen. Our own patient and steady desire to grow, fed by the love and kindness of others, will not be stopped by anything or anyone. Our own gentleness is a powerful force in our lives. It is like the gentle bush that grows through granite.

What can I gain by gentleness today?

June 14

Fear not that life shall come to an end,
but rather fear that it shall never have a
beginning.

— J. H. Newman

Our fears lock us up if we let them. They can prevent us from tasting adventure, from experiencing new wonders. We are often terrified of unknowns and fret about what might happen if we try something new. We worry if new people will like us — if we'll fit in.

It is natural to be cautious about the unknown, and anything new is just that. But we can keep our caution from becoming fear by taking action, with the faith that we never encounter anything we can't handle in some way.

Unknowns are merely joys we haven't met. We hold the keys to our own cages and can free ourselves when we use our courage and inner strength to overcome our fears.

What new joy can I discover beneath my fear today?

*Bad moments, like good ones, tend to
be grouped together.*
                              —Edna O'Brien

Once in a while, we have days when we think
the whole world is against us. A parent has repri-
manded us, a brother broke our new game, or the
teacher at school disciplined the whole class. We
sometimes let our thoughts center on a cluster of
bad moments and forget the good moments of the
day.

We shouldn't forget about the two ducks we fed
part of our sandwich to, the friend who made us
laugh, or the gym teacher who praised the whole
class. Deciding to think about these good moments
can allow our spirits to rise and make the bad
moments fade away.

After all, if life were all good moments, we
would take them for granted. Let us accept the bad
ones gratefully, then, as opportunities to appreciate the good.

What good moments can I remember right now?

June 16

*Being alive is being creative. You need
do nothing but affirm your aliveness.*
—Gay Bonner

What does it mean to be alive? Does it mean
merely breathing, eating, and moving around, or
is there more to it? Being alive can mean different
things to different people. To some, it's sewing a
baby quilt for a new life about to be born. To
others, it's singing, or walking, or running. Still
others find it in the exhilaration of skiing, or the
tropical splendor they find when scuba diving.

Each of us has our own favorite activity that lets
us feel our creativity and vitality, that lets us feel a
part of the larger world. Two gifts these activities
leave us with are joy and energy. Joy is one of the
most creative forces we can call on, and energy
gives us the power to do it well.

What will my creative activity be today?

You will jump to it someday. Then you'll fly. You'll really fly. After that you'll quite simply, quite calmly make your own stones, your own floor plan, your own sound.

—Anne Sexton

A young man sat beside a whispering creek all day for years, never moving. The townsfolk who watched him wondered whether he heard the gurgling creek sounds, or felt the sting of insects, or saw the racoons when they came at night to sip from the cool, dark waters.

One day the young man rose and dashed up the hill above the creek. There, using all the healing strength of the stream which he had quietly absorbed over the years, he gathered stones. He arranged them layer by layer to fit the plan he had thought out by the creek, and feverishly he built his home. When done, he let out a brassy, booming holler of joy. Imagine the townsfolk's surprise when they turned their eyes to that lonely spot by the creek and saw a huge castle of stone above the place where the young man once rested.

What plans can I make during my idle hours today?

June 18

Let your conscience be your guide.
—*Jiminy Cricket*

Crickets sing on summer nights because it's their nature to do so. They don't think about whistling or trumpeting or sleeping or changing the world. They've figured out their role on earth, and they do it.

We are a bit more complex than crickets, and most of the time that's lucky. In most of our affairs it's our conscience more than sheer instinct that helps us choose those thoughts and acts and feelings that are right for us.

Each of us has that little voice inside, relentless as a chirping cricket, telling us what to do. Even in the middle of our toughest decisons, we always have within us the solution that is right for us. All we have to do is listen — and trust.

What does my inner voice say about today's decisions?

Jealousy is cruel as the grave.
—Song of Solomon

Most bushes and small trees need trimming every year. They have branches that hang out over the sidewalk and get in people's way. Sometimes the branches grow so long and low to the ground that the tree looks weighted down.

Jealousy is like an overgrown branch — it weighs us down. It is one of those feelings all of us deal with. We may be jealous of someone's looks or talent, or maybe even their good luck. Like the overgrown branches, jealousy sticks out all over and gets in other people's way as well as our own. It is a part of us we need to keep cutting back.

If we are good gardeners, we will get out the clippers. Seeing and talking about our jealousy is the best way to start using those clippers. If we do this, our own leaves will be healthier, and our blossoms will grow.

Is there someone I am jealous of? Can I use my clippers today?

June 20

The most valuable thing we can do for the psyche, occasionally, is to let it rest, wander, live in the changing light of a room, not to try to do or be anything whatsoever.

—May Sarton

A whole world can be seen through even the smallest window. Knowing this can help us slow down and enjoy everyday events. We can listen to the regular rhythms of letter carriers and school children, dogs and delivery trucks, city buses and song birds playing out a piece of their daily lives outside the window.

We can greet the letter carrier who comes up the walk, feed the robin who lands on the sill, wave to the kids who've found a shortcut through our backyards on their way home from school.

It is not necessary, today, for us to fill our lives with important meetings, gala parties, expensive treats, toys, or outings to be happy. There is a whole world to be discovered just outside the nearest window.

What worlds lie on the other side of my window today?

*To be able to invite pain to join in my
experience and not have to control my
life to avoid pain is such a freedom!*
　　　　　　　　　　—Christina Baldwin

If we really stopped to think about it, we would
be astounded to discover how much of our time is
spent trying to avoid pain. We are afraid to say
what we think or tell others our needs because we
fear rejection. We are afraid to face the pain of our
own anger. We are afraid of telling others who we
are. When we are afraid of opening up to others
for fear they will hurt us, we are not free, we are
prisoners of our own fears.

Pain is a natural part of life, and we are gifted
with the ability to feel it. Pain teaches us, makes us
work harder sometimes, and it helps us appreciate
pleasure.

When we accept pain, and stop exhausting ourselves trying to avoid it, we will be free to live life
more fully and without so much worry.

How has my own fear limited my freedom?

June 22

> *When fate hands us a lemon, let's try to*
> *make lemonade.*
> —Dale Carnegie

Good fortune is built on misfortune. By losing a race we learn what mistakes to avoid next time we run. A burglar may make us install the lock that will keep out a murderer. Each time a toddler falls is a lesson in how to walk.

We can never assume that, because things are not going the way we want, they are not following a better plan. God is a better manager than we can hope to be. If things aren't shaping up the way we like, let's wait with curiosity to see what better things are in store for us. Let's look for lights in the darkness and follow them to the bright day that always will follow. We will remember our lessons of misfortune with gratitude.

What can I learn from delay today?

Real friends are those who, when you've made a fool of yourself, don't feel that you've done a permanent job.
—*Erwin T. Randall*

What kind of friends do we have? Are they people who complain a lot? Are they people who laugh at us or put others down?

The kind of people we want to be will decide what kind of friends we have. If we want to feel sorry for ourselves, we will choose friends who will tell us how rotten their lives are. If we want to think we're better than others, we will hang around people who laugh at others' mistakes.

But if we want to be the best we can be, we will pick friends who see the good in life, people who will encourage us to be ourselves and who will help us try harder at things that are difficult for us.

How can I be a better friend today?

June 24

Self-image sets the boundaries of individual accomplishment.
—Maxwell Maltz

The way we think about ourselves determines how we behave and who we become. If Eileen believes she is good at baseball, she will swing the bat more confidently and catch fly balls more easily. And her extra effort will generally pay off. At math, Steve thinks he's a whiz and it makes him proud. He studies so he'll continue to be a whiz.

The image we have of ourselves is like the blueprint the contractor follows when building a house. When we see ourselves sad or angry, our behavior and personality will match it. When we see ourselves withdrawn and afraid, we seem to avoid activities that involve others. How wonderful that we can change our behavior and thus ourselves by changing the picture we carry in our minds.

Do I have a good picture of myself today?

It is good to have an end to journey towards, but it is the journey that matters, in the end.

—Ursula K. LeGuin

Billy and his dad were excited about fan appreciation night. They wanted to get one of the souvenir baseballs thrown into the stands. As they hurried toward their seats, they saw a man drop a ten-dollar bill. Billy picked up the money.

"Hey, Mister," he said loudly. The man in front of him turned around. "You dropped this." Billy handed him the money.

"Thank you," said the man. Billy returned to his dad. Just as they reached their row, a ball came sailing towards their empty seats. Someone from the row behind caught it. Billy swallowed hard.

"I know," said his dad, looking at Billy. "But you did the right thing."

For his effort, Billy will bring home a souvenir far more lasting and valuable than a baseball or a ten-dollar bill. He will know the bittersweet feeling of making a sacrifice to do what is right.

What sacrifice have I made to do what is right?

June 26

> *One cricket said to another —*
> *come, let us be ridiculous, and say*
> *love!*
>
> —Conrad Aiken

Let's all sit in a circle and take turns being ridiculous about what our love is like. Let's play tag with it, and pass it on. Let's say that our love is like diamonds sprinkled on a clear moonless sky, and let's pass it on. Let's say it's like one rose petal too tender to touch, and let's pass it on. Let's say it's like rainbows filling a city sky, and pass it on. Let's say it's small and hard, like an agate or shell, and let's keep passing it on.

We can find images for love all around us, and when we express it to others this way, it grows.

What is my love like today?

*When one door of happiness closes, an-
other opens; but often we look so long
at the closed door that we do not see
the one which has been opened for us.*
— *Helen Keller*

In the game of musical chairs, everyone walks around a circle of chairs. When the music stops, they scramble for the nearest open chair. If we were playing this game and found the nearest chairs taken, wouldn't we quickly look around for the next open one? To remain immobilized, angry that the chair we wanted was taken, would un- doubtedly lose our place in the game.

Sometimes in life, we set our sights on a particu- lar chair. Perhaps there is an award we want to win, or we want to be the high scorer on our team. Perhaps there is a promotion or a job we would like to get. When we do not get what we want, it is easy to keep looking at what we didn't get instead of seeing all we have.

It is important to be grateful for what we have — for the open doors and empty chairs waiting and inviting our attention. Loss and disappoint- ment are a part of life — but the music will play again and our lives can move on.

What is available to me today?

June 28

It's the deepest channel that runs most true.

—Kate Wolf

The greatest rivers spread themselves out wide and lazy over the earth. They roll over on themselves like great turtles turning in the warm sun. A river flows, drawn to the oceans, carving ever-deepening channels, nestling snug in the earth's welcoming lap. The current is strongest in the deepest channel. Boat navigators know that finding that channel means finding the swiftest current and the safest voyage home.

When we look at a river, or at another person, we see only the surface. What keeps our attention is usually some movement or activity on the surface. But there is more than meets the eye, especially to people. When we overlook someone because that person is quiet or simple, we may be robbing ourselves of an eye-opening discovery.

Which deeper things can I look for in my day?

Let us open our natures, throw wide the
doors of our hearts and let in the sun-
shine of good will and kindness.
— *O. S. Marden*

Kindness is among the gifts we can most easily spread among others. The more we give of kind words and deeds, the more we discover that kindness is like a burning candle which lights many other candles without losing a trace of its own brightness. Our kindnesses are assets which return unexpected dividends when we invest them in the happiness of others. Kindness is the very basis of love. It softens the most severe anger and gladdens the hardest hearts.

No kindness is too small to win and hold the affection of others because it is made up of gentleness, love, generosity, unselfishness, and caring.

What kindness do I have to offer today?

June 30

Cultivate your garden. Let it take root
in you until your thousand eyes open
like violets to morning light.
                              —Nancy Paddock

In our imaginations, we can mix images and ideas from all over the world — imagine the thousand eyes of a peacock growing among the purple violets, or babies that grow on trees! In our imaginations we can also nurture feelings of love, affection, self-esteem.

All of us — not just writers — can learn to see the images in our own minds. We can do this by breathing slowly, relaxing, and looking at the movie in our minds. We may see a field of wildflowers, or find ourselves wading across a stream in the mountains. We might see happiness as wildflowers and grass coming up through the sidewalk, breaking the concrete into chunks and sand, growing so slowly yet with such great power. It may help us appreciate our growth today to look at it this way.

Can I visualize my happiness right now? What does it look like?

July

*Those who contemplate the beauty of
the earth find reserves of strength that
will endure as long as life lasts.*
                    —*Rachel Carson*

Beauty is everywhere. It is in the daisies, in the lavender wildflowers, in the new green grass of Spring. As we walk through life, noticing such beauty strengthens us. It reminds us of the spiritual creative force alive in this world. On better days, we can feel our own creativity gaining power from such beauty. On harder days, nature's sunset can help us step out of our suffering for a moment to be comforted and inspired by its splendor.

Even storms, in their wild and angry way, show us a power greater than ourselves. Such awesome beauty is beyond our understanding, and yet it is part of the earth we live on.

What lessons will nature teach me today?

July 2

Now my soul hath elbow room.
—William Shakespeare

If we spend too much time together we are bound to grow weary of one another. This would happen regardless of who the other person was. In a family, we need some time apart to pursue other interests and friendships. We may be able to meet many needs for each other, but there will be some we cannot meet. If we press too hard upon one another we will cramp our life together.

Our needs for space aren't just physical. Freedom to think and feel what seems appropriate for us, to be alone if we want, is a large part of our lives together. Only with this kind of freedom is love possible. Love requires freedom. We need to value each other, and at the same time realize that no one person or family can fill us with all life has to offer.

What are my own freedoms at home?

You are here for a purpose. There is not a duplicate of you in the whole wide world; there never has been, there never will be. You were brought here now to fill a certain need. Take time to think that over.

—Lou Austin

No other person is exactly like you or me. No one can do exactly what we can, or touch another person in exactly the way we can. Out of all the people who could have been created, we were chosen to be a part of this time and place.

We are needed to fulfill a plan, in our families as well as in other relationships. Knowing we have unique abilities, we will spend less time feeling jealous of what others can do.

Through our dreams and yearnings, God shows us who we can be. It is up to us to have the courage to follow that dream with action.

What unique gift can I offer the world today?

July 4

> *In Micronesian, there's a word,* kukaro, *which has no corresponding word in English. When people say they are going to* kukaro, *they mean they are going to relax, sit around, hang out. They are* being, *not* doing.
> —Eli and Beth Halpern

As children, our best times are often trips to an amusement park, fishing at the lake, camping, or just sitting idly under a tree. These make the best memories, and times sitting around a campfire roasting marshmallows or having a root beer after a family outing seem to bring out the love we share.

We don't seem to be accomplishing anything at these times. No chores are getting done around the house, no schoolwork, no repairs, no money-making.

But these times of peace, relaxation, and a sense of endless time of being, not doing, may be essential to our ability to get other things done later. Certainly we are most receptive to our feelings, new ideas, and unplanned adventures at these moments. Maybe we should add *kukaro* to our vocabulary.

What timeless thing can I do today?

In uplifting, get underneath.
                    —George Ade

A sandpile in the summer is deceiving. The top-most sand burns hot on our feet. But as we push down toward the center, we come to a damp, cool place that soothes and oozes between our toes.

The nature of most things is not revealed at the surface. Like the sandpile, many people and situations we encounter are, on the surface, downright uncomfortable. The reward is in digging deeper — to the essential goodness, the core or meaning, the true friend. It takes time, a little knowledge, and abundant trust that we will not be burned.

What have I discovered by digging a little lately?

July 6

> *Forgiveness is all-powerful. Forgiveness heals all ills.*
>
> —*Catherine Ponder*

Getting mad at someone, a friend perhaps, is normal. Everybody gets mad sometimes. But when we stay mad for very long, it ruins all the fun we'd planned on having throughout the day. Staying mad multiplies. Sometimes it seems we are mad at the dog, our mom, another friend, even the TV.

Forgiving the people we're mad at works like magic. We don't even have to forgive them out loud. We can forgive them in our own minds. The result is the same. Pretty soon the whole day looks bright again. When we're mad, we are the ones who suffer most.

Who can I forgive today, and make my day a better one?

I found words to every thought I ever
had, but one. . . .
                    —Emily Dickinson

What kinds of thoughts can't be put into words?
We feel lost in space, mind-boggled by how small
and big the stars are. We are sure and unsure about
death, its blank and steady stare. Or we have done
something that makes us feel both good and bad.
Sometimes we hate someone we love, but we aren't
sure what hate is, or love. We are scared of crowds
and afraid of being abandoned, always alone.
Sometimes we just want to laugh and cry, and
when words fail we expect someone to know what
our silences mean.

What are some ways I try to express my feelings
without using words?

July 8

> *Hurry, hurry has no blessing.*
> —*Swahili Proverb*

In a busy family there is a lot of activity. We sometimes feel imprisoned by all the work, school, extracurricular activities, housework, meetings, and special events. In the press to do it all, we may lose our peace because of the hurry. We rush to eat; we rush to work; we rush to get there on time. Much of this cannot be helped. But hurry has no blessing, as the proverb goes. We can create quick tempers and a lot of frustration if we try to hurry too much.

When we allow enough time to slow things down, we give ourselves a chance to enjoy what we're doing, and to develop along spiritual lines. Inner peace depends on our keeping a balance in all the things we do. Only then can we feel the joy that comes from having enough time to do things quietly and smoothly, and value the inner peace that comes when we do not hurry.

How can I take my time today and enjoy myself?

*A mother is not a person to lean on,
but a person to make leaning unneces-
sary.*
                        —*Dorothy Canfield Fisher*

A strong, healthy tree is one which is free to
grow straight and tall. A weak tree often must lean
against another for support. It is not that different
with people. We are not healthy and strong when
we must always lean on another to support us.

This doesn't mean it isn't healthy to accept help.
But the best help we can get or give is that which
enables us to do things without it. Sometimes we
think we lose a relationship when others don't
need our help, or when we don't need theirs all the
time. The reverse is true. Only when we are each
strong enough to stand on our own can we really
share the kind of help which allows both helped
and helper to be independent.

Have I been giving the right kind of help?

July 10

What a man thinks of himself, that is which determines, or rather indicates, his fate.
—Henry David Thoreau

Let us think of ourselves as made of dust, and allow us to be as proud of it as if it were true. For dust is everywhere. We see it in solemn rooms streaked by sun, dancing like fine angels in a cathedral light. It is the stuff of life. And it drifts down on fancy tables where the richest people eat. It cannot be denied a place. And it returns time and time again like the seasons. It is one of the wonders of the world. And when no one sees or cares, it finds a secret corner in which to keep a solitary peace. It intends no harm. We find it at home on old leather books, the ones that preserve our noblest thoughts.

And from where we stand, it seems that even the stars are made of it. When we feel low, unworthy, or useless, let's remember that these feelings are only a small but important part of us, that even great things are made of small parts, and that we, as whole beings, are always greater than the sum of these parts.

What feelings am I made of today?

*Always think of what you have to do
as easy and it will become so.*
                        —Emile Corie

How we think about the activities before us is
very important. If we think cleaning the garage is
hard, dirty, and no chance for fun, that's just how
it will feel. We'll be tired before we even begin.
However, if we approach it like a treasure hunt,
expecting to rediscover some long-forgotten treasures, we'll enjoy the task. In fact, it will feel like a
game.

The thoughts we carry in our minds determine
whether our tasks are fun or not. What good fortune it is that we can control those thoughts. If we
approach an assignment for school or a job believing that we're able to do it, that it's not too hard for
us, we'll finish with ease. Our thoughts determine
our successes. In this way, our lives are in our own
hands.

How much better can I make my life today?

July 12

We love the things we love for what they are.

—Robert Frost

Once there was a little girl who had a stuffed frog named Jeremy. Jeremy went everywhere with the girl — to imaginary picnics with her other dolls, to school, on trips, and, once, even into the bathtub! Every night, Jeremy slept cradled in her arms.

Over time, Jeremy grew old and tattered. He had lost an eye, and he limped because the girl used to use one of his legs as a handle, and it had gotten crushed. His nose was a little mangled too, from being dragged on the ground.

But the girl loved that frog, no matter how bedraggled he looked. And he never did anything. He was just always there. He was just Jeremy, and she loved him for that.

Today, that girl is a young woman and has outgrown childish things. But in her bedroom, you'll still find Jeremy, tattered and repaired, asleep on her bed. She still loves him dearly, for what he is.

Who do I love, and why?

*When you have to make a choice and
don't make it, that is in itself a choice.*
—William James

There are times when it's hard to make a decision. When we go to the fair, for instance, we may
want to do more things than we have time for, so
we don't know what plans to make. Waiting to
decide until we see what the fair has to offer is one
choice. Not deciding because we're afraid of what
may happen is also a choice. We may find ourselves thinking so much about what could happen
that we miss all the exciting things going on
around us.

It's necessary to keep in mind that any course of
action is a decision, but no decision is irreversible.
We are free to do what we decide, and are freed by
the awareness that whatever we do is based on our
own decision and no one else's.

*What important decisions shall I make without
fear today?*

July 14

*Happiness is not a matter of events; it
depends upon the tides of the mind.*
—Alice Meyvell

It's thought that Abe Lincoln once said, "We're
as happy as we make up our minds to be." In other
words, we decide to be happy. Bad weather, lost
toys, broken plans, even angry friends don't have
to ruin our own happiness unless we let them.
We're always in control of our own thoughts and
feelings, and happiness is a feeling we can choose
even when others around us have chosen to be
angry or sad. Even when the day is gloomy and
none of our plans are working out, we can still be
cheerful if we decide to be. How lucky we are that
someone else can't decide for us how to feel. We'd
be nothing more than robots if that were true.

Am I ready to make this day a happy one?

*I was forced to live far beyond my years
when just a child. Now I have reversed
the order and I intend to remain young
indefinitely.*

—Mary Pickford

We can all learn to change our lives so the child within each of us can live in balance with the people we have become. We can learn to give the child a voice, let the child play, let the child express needs and fears and pleasures.

We might look at our old baby pictures for a valuable lesson. We will see pictures of ourselves on rocking horses, grinning and waving; pictures of ourselves with our most precious toy — a crude metal car, perhaps; pictures of ourselves rolling in the grass. The lesson we learn is that it doesn't take much to make this child happy — even today.

We keep our own happiness safe inside us to call on whenever we need it, as long as we keep a healthy relationship with the child within. When we nourish the child, we can be assured the child will also nourish us.

What simple thing will make me happy today?

July 16

Let a joy keep you. Reach out your hands and take it when it runs by.
—*Carl Sandburg*

There is a song that says joy is like the rain. It comes across our window pane and then goes away again. When joy comes knocking at our window we can reach out and let it in. Joy comes to us in many ways — through deep laughter, through games played together in a spirit of fun and sharing. Singing together, skating, and being around a campfire are all ways we share joy. Yet joy can also be felt alone.

Each moment of joy we reach for strengthens our spirits. Joyful memories can sustain us through days of long hard work. Like rain, joy comes and goes, yet its nourishment keeps our spirits alive.

How can I share my joy today?

When you feel rejected, start accepting yourself, and then go out and accept someone.

—Sondra Ray

There was once a mother who felt rejected when her children grew up and needed to separate from her. She felt hurt when they pushed her away and no longer wanted all the love and caring that she wanted to give them. She thought, What's wrong with me?

Encouraged by her friends, she began to ask herself another question: What's right with me? The more answers she found to that question, the better she liked herself. The better she liked herself, the more she was able to see her children's need to separate from her as their own natural and healthy urge for independence, and not the result of her shortcomings.

Our good points may seem undesirable to others, but that's not our fault. Sometimes, too much of a good thing can be inappropriate, but that doesn't make it bad.

What's right with me today?

July 18

The great end of life is not knowledge but action.

—Thomas Huxley

Sometimes we have good ideas about how to make things better. We might know we need to spend more quality time with others. We might know it would be better if mealtime was not so hectic and really became a time for sharing the day's events. Knowing what needs to happen is part of the process of change. But we have to put that knowledge into action.

All our good intentions, no matter what they may be, do not really mean anything until we move into action. A hug is better than a thought of love; a story read together is better than a wonderful vacation that did not get past the planning stage, just as a finished house is something we can live in, while the blueprint is soon forgotten. When we act on our ideas, we put ourselves into the world as a force for change.

What change can I set loose in the world today?

Trust takes time. If you don't invest it,
then you don't get it.

—Anonymous

Trusting other human beings is like planting a garden. First we must choose where to plant — is the soil healthy, is it open to sunlight? We would not plant seeds on rocks that are hard and ungiving. In the same way, we need to choose friends who are trustworthy, who are like rich soil open to planting and sunlight.

Then we need to plant the seeds of time and care. If we share some of our feelings and are welcomed, we will know it is safe to share more. We can share ourselves in our own time — even a garden grows slowly, and can take only so much sun and rain in one day.

Having trust in someone feeds the spirit. Trust also gives us the courage to be beautiful, like the flowers of our gardens.

Am I brave enough to trust others, and to be worthy of their trust?

July 20

It is terribly amusing how many different climates of feeling one can go through in a day.
—Anne Morrow Lindbergh

When we travel by canoe down a river we can notice the changes that take place. In one spot the river is wide and the water moves slowly. Around the next bend the river narrows and the current speeds up. Ahead of us we see rapids waiting to test our skill.

Our feelings can also change as quickly as the river. We may have times in our day when we feel good about ourselves. Then, all of a sudden, someone may tease us about something. We begin to feel like the scared canoeist shooting the rapids for the first time. How wonderful it is to know that we are never given a test we can't handle, that everything that happens in our lives is for the sake of our growth, and that we are watched over at all times by God.

How can I use today's obstacles for my own growth?

*Dependency (on another human being)
is the inability to experience wholeness
or to function adequately without the
certainty that one is being actively
cared for by another.*

—M. Scott Peck

No matter what we may think, overdependence
on another can be very unloving because it drains
others of any chance for personal growth. Those
of us who have been dependent on other people
are so busy acquiring love that we ourselves have
no energy left to truly give love. It's as if we're
starving, and scrambling for every little bit of love
we can find, with no thought to offering it to others. No wonder they often quickly get tired of us.

We can't force or expect others to do things with
us, talk to us, or love us. The way to be surely
loved is to be worthy of it. We can work at being
worthy by exercising our freedom to feel and do
things without others' permission, and to allow
them the same opportunity.

What can I do on my own today?

July 22

A good laugh heals a lot of hurts.
—Madeleine L'Engle

The ability to laugh at ourselves has always been important. In old days, fools and jesters held an important place in the royal courts. Today we have clowns who make us laugh.

If we look closely at a clown's face, we will often notice a bit of sadness around the eyes. Clowns are able to move easily from sad expressions to ones full of delight very easily. For all of us, laughter and tears come from the same deep well inside. And often, after a good cry, we find ourselves ready to laugh, easily and joyfully.

Laughter is a gift waiting for us on the other side of our sadness.

Can I begin to laugh by smiling now?

There is no reality except the one contained within us.

—Herman Hesse

Claude Gellee painted lovely pictures of the English countryside. Europeans loved his landscapes, with their blue hues and mild distortions. But when the people went for the carriage rides in the country, they were disappointed because it didn't look the way Gellee had painted it. Then someone discovered that if you held blue glass up to your eyes and looked through it, the trees and hills and sky looked just like a Gellee painting! Soon everyone was looking through "Claude glasses" when they travelled.

We often let others do our seeing for us. We get lazy and rely on the images of television and movies, instead of really seeing with our own eyes. Our world becomes distorted and we lose sight of the natural beauty that surrounds us.

Each of us carries reality inside ourselves, and as we grow stronger within, we discover that we can see clearest when we trust our own eyes. There is a glorious world, full and rich, just waiting for us to glimpse it.

Will I see the world through my own eyes today?

July 24

I had crossed the line. I was free: but there was no one to welcome me to the land of freedom. I was a stranger in a strange land.

—Harriet Tubman

Harriet Tubman was a Black woman who devoted her life to helping slaves escape their bondage. In her youth, she had been hit on the head so she suffered dizzy spells for the rest of her life. In spite of this, and at great risk to her own life, she guided many slaves on the Underground Railroad to freedom.

Freedom from slavery is different today but just as necessary. It may mean freedom from being a slave to what others think of us, freedom from eating more than is healthy for us, freedom from jealousy, freedom from trying to force others to do what we want them to do.

We are free to be the very best persons we can be. Our own freedom can be even more fulfilling when we welcome others enthusiastically into that land of freedom by allowing them the room to be themselves without fear of judgment. In this way, by freeing ourselves, we free one another.

How can I free myself today?

*He wanted to hold onto his fury, to
guard it like a treasure. He would not
let it be stolen from him. . . . But already, he felt it slipping, softened by
Ben's compassionate touch.*
—Joe Johnston and Nilo Rodis-Jamero

The glassblower is an artist who takes broken
glass and melts it in a very hot furnace. Then the
glassblower blows through a long tube and creates
objects such as cups and plates and pieces of art.

The sharp edges of our anger are like pieces of
broken glass. We all have things in our lives that
anger us — it is only human to bump into our
sharp edges. One edge might be crabby, another
silent and withdrawn, and still another yelling and
screaming.

The heat of love and compassion can melt our
anger. This may take the form of sympathy for
ourselves, or for the people we love. More often, it
is the compassion of those around us that helps
melt our anger. Sometimes saying I'm sorry is a
good way to melt anger and find the love underneath it.

What beauty can I create with my anger today?

Isn't it great life is open-ended!
—Brigitte Frase

Elizabeth Lawton, known as "Grandma Lawton," is an American artist who never drew a picture until she was sixty-eight years old. She spent all the years before that time trying to cope with depression. She had gone through therapy, medications, and shock treatment and continued to be severely depressed. But then she signed up for an art class and the act of drawing cured her depression. She continues to make fabulous pictures.

What does she think about the critical acclaim her artwork has received? She says she wants others to know about her art so it may give hope to those who have also "suffered from feelings."

Many of us have suffered from feelings. We must remember that we can each turn to our creativity — at any age — as a source for our well-being. All we need to do is have faith in the potential goodness within ourselves and those we love.

What creative activity can I look to for comfort today?

In summer I am very glad
We children are so small,
For we can see a thousand things
That men can't see at all.
—Laurence Alma-Tadema

Out behind the house a little boy is turning over stepping stones which form the sidewalk. Underneath these stones he has discovered many different kinds of worms and bugs. They wiggle this way and that when their cover is removed. He is only four, but he is the only one in the family who has made this discovery.

In a child's eyes there are many wonderful things which escape the attention of the adult world. In order to see them, we must often take the time to let those younger than us show the way. Even though we may have lost our own childlike view of the world, others can guide us and thereby enrich our lives. We have much to teach and share with each other, regardless of our ages.

What can I learn from one younger than me today?

July 28

One law for lion and ox is oppression.
—William Blake

What would the forest be like if deer, squirrel, and owl alike were required to sleep only at noon? Or the sky, if all birds were forced by law to fly in lines? Or the sea, if all fish had to stay forever in schools? We all know a lion and an ox, and we've all acted like a chicken, jackass, goat, or fox. Now and then we're slow or fast, bright or dull, willing or not.

So when others go the way we know we must go, we will follow the same law. But we don't have to be as others are, just to avoid being thought "strange." How truly strange life would be if everyone were the same. We have our own way, our own good time, our own free laws to discover and obey.

Will I need to obey someone else's rules if I govern myself well?

A good marriage is that in which each appoints the other guardian of his solitude.

—*Rainer Maria Rilke*

Solitude is vital to our well-being, but in a family it's hard sometimes to find the space and time to be alone. The house is often crowded with laughter, voices, the radio, and the TV. There are often many things going on at the same time.

It's true that our family is a team, and that we work together, whether we intend to or not, to create the environment we live in. If it's noisy, that's the way we live. Noise is life to some. The fact that others need our help or company is wonderful proof of our value. But if we can be guardians of each other's solitude, out of love for one another, we will each come back renewed, strengthened, and recreated. We can bring new life into our days when we are alone with ourselves and God.

How can I help someone find rest and renewal today?

July 30

The hopeful man sees success where others see failure, sunshine where others see shadows and storm.
—*O. S. Marden*

When wise men say, "Hope springs eternal," they are reminding us that, no matter how great are the obstacles, the hope of winning out in the long run still exists. Hope is our friend when all else has failed. When we have strength of character and an energetic mind, hope always flourishes.

We discover that, at the very brink of despair, we will find courage to keep trying as long as there is hope for success. After all, what have we got to lose? Without hope, we have no chance, anyway. Our chance for glory comes when we keep trying even though all seems lost. Our hearts remain strong and brave when hope reminds us that challenges last until a game is over.

What light of hope can I keep burning within me today?

*Sometimes it's worse to win a fight than
to lose.*
                              —*Billie Holiday*

We all see things differently. It is part of the
wonderful variety of the world that we all have
different points of view. We've all seen baseball
players arguing with an umpire over a close call,
but, in order to play the game, they must accept
the umpire's judgment.

When we stubbornly refuse to let friends or family members speak their ideas simply because we
disagree with them, we risk the loss of a friend or
the understanding of a family member. It is when
we allow others to disagree that we take a step
forward — a step that opens our ears and our
hearts to all sorts of people and ideas.

How well can I accept other's opinions today?

August

Flying is largely a matter of having the right attitude — plus, of course, good wing feathers.

—*E. B. White*

The swan flies with majesty, confidence, and grace. It is made to fly, of course, but it learns as much about flying from its parents as it knows by instinct. It is not born with the ability to fly, but with the potential.

Each of us is born with the potential to fly in many skies. We may sing or dance or write or run, fix machines, teach children, speak, listen, sympathize. And we can do all these things well, as only humans can. It is not the *ability* to do these things that makes us human, it's what we *do* with that ability.

Knowing how to prepare ourselves before we spread our wings is part of discovering what we can do. When we learn to ride a bike, we *know* we can do it; our parent's hand on the seat helps us know it.

Wanting to soar is the first part of flight; it is studying, practicing, and asking for help that allows us to get off the ground.

What steps can I take today toward reaching my potential?

August 2

> *Happiness is a mental habit, a mental attitude, and if it is not learned and practiced in the present it is never experienced.*
>
> —*Maxwell Maltz*

If only I had a new bike, then I'd be happy. If only my family were more understanding, then I'd be happy. If only my hair were styled better. If only I had more friends. If only. . . . Sometimes we begin to sound like a broken record when things go wrong, so certain that if the events and conditions of our lives were different, we'd be happy.

It's an old and unfortunate habit that we look around outside ourselves for happiness. We can never be sure of it if we count on certain conditions to guarantee it. However, we can always be sure of happiness if we carry it with us wherever we go. The happiness habit can be developed, with practice, just as surely as good piano playing or accurate pitching. We can control our own thoughts. The decision to make them happy ones is ours to make.

Am I carrying my happiness within me right now?

*Creativity is so delicate a flower that
praise tends to make it bloom, while
discouragement often nips it in the bud.*
　　　　　　　　　　　—Alex Osborn

A garden of flowers blooming is a beautiful
sight to see. Through the green leaves surrounding
a tulip we see hints of yellow or pink or red. Each
day the flowers greet us with their radiant color.
Yet, a sudden frost would wilt and fade the
flowers.

Each time we create something new with our
talents we are like a young flower opening.
Whether we draw or write or sew or play a musical
instrument, all creativity has this in common. Appreciation from those around us is like sunshine
for the flowers. Harsh criticism, however, is like
the cold air — it wilts and deadens our desire to
create.

We all need warm encouragement for our en-
deavors, and we can give as well as receive it. In
this way, creativity can bloom in our homes and
our friendships, bringing a garden full of color and
delight into our lives.

*What encouragement can I offer to someone near
me?*

August 4

Do I love you because you're beautiful
Or are you beautiful because
*   I love you?*
                    —Oscar Hammerstein

Once, a powerful king agreed to help a small, lost boy find his mother. Since the boy described his mother as the most beautiful woman in the world, the king commanded all the beautiful women in the kingdom to come to the castle.

From miles around, they came — women with complexions of porcelain and hair of spun gold, with cheeks the color of apricots and eyes as dark as the raven's. But none of them was the boy's mother. When the last of the women had paraded before them, and the king and the boy had begun to despair, they heard a timid knock on the door. "Come in," the king said wearily. In shuffled an old washer woman, her grey hair tied up in a kerchief, her hands rough and red, her dress coarse and patched.

"Mother!" the boy cried when he saw her, and he leapt from his chair and raced into the woman's arms. The king stared in amazement.

Will I be able to see the real beauty in others today?

There is surely a piece of divinity in us, something that was before the elements. . . .
                              —Sir Thomas Browne

One definition of *divinity* in the dictionary is "supreme excellence." It also means "god-like character" and "divine nature."

Doesn't that describe someone we love? When we are in love with someone, we see only the best of that person — it's impossible to see anything else. That person is "divine," we say, perfect for us, because he or she loves us and is lovable.

Each one of us has a part that is divine. We see it occasionally in others, and they see it in us when they love us. We can draw on that divine part of every person for strength and hope and courage and faith and love. There is wonderful, mysterious beauty in all of us, even when we behave badly.

What divinity do I see in those around me right now?

August 6

> *What matters?. . .Only the flicker of*
> *light within the darkness, the feeling of*
> *warmth within the cold, the knowledge*
> *of love within the void.*
> —*Joan Walsh Anglund*

If we were lost at sea, surrounded by darkness pierced only by one distant blinking light, we would follow that light. As we followed it, it would become clearer and brighter until it brought us safely to land.

Sometimes when we're depressed, we feel as though we're lost on a dark sea. But there is always a flicker of light for us. It may be prayer, or the love of a special friend. When we see that light, we need to move toward it. Whatever brings us hope is like that flicker of light. The more we seek it, the clearer and brighter the light will become.

When we are cold and our bodies begin to numb, we must keep moving. Movement will keep us alive. When our emotions are numb, we need people or things or places that will warm our hearts. When no one else is around, hot baths or a favorite treat can bring the warmth of our own self-love into our lives when we need it the most.

How can I brighten my inner light today?

*Love consists in this, that two solitudes
protect and touch and greet each other.*
—Rainer Maria Rilke

For a relationship to be healthy and fulfilling,
each of us must respect the other. "Two solitudes"
is exactly what we are, and we will never be one,
no matter how close we become. It may feel like
that at times, but we always remain separate persons with our own thoughts, feelings, dreams, and
interests.

When we love one another, we allow each other
to be who we are, to have our own lives, for it is
out of those separate lives that we bring strength
and energy and life into our relationships.

We are meant to honor the differences between
us. Often these differences lead to squabbles, but
when we recognize that each of us is necessary to
the union we have created, we create a better one,
far superior to the sum of its parts.

*What differences between us make our lives to-
gether better?*

August 8

*The important thing is not to conquer
but to have fought at all.*
                    —Olympic motto

People come from all over the world to partici-
pate in the Olympics, and they come with a wide
range of talent. A lot of them know they will not
win a medal, yet they have trained hard for their
event. They meet people from all corners of the
earth who love the same activity.

There is a contagious joy and excitement the
athletes share in their time together. It is a sense
that the sharing of worldwide joy and peace is
indeed possible.

Whether we succeed or fail in what we do is not
the essential thing. What is important is the heart
with which we live our lives.

*If I could share something with the world, what
would it be?*

*What is without periods of rest will not
endure.*

—Ovid

When we are tired, we need to stop and give
ourselves time to rest. Sometimes we think we
can't spare the time. But without rest, all our activity soon becomes a burden and there is no joy in it.
Animals know it is necessary to take time to rest.
This is part of the rhythm of life: activity and rest,
effort and relaxation.

Our bad moods are often our body's way of
telling us we need rest. When we were little, we
needed naps. Somehow, we forget to allow ourselves this right when we are older. We are wise to
remember we never outgrow this need for rest to
make the day go better.

When we return to our day refreshed, we have
given ourselves and all those around us the gift of
ourselves at our best.

What can I do better when I am rested?

August 10

It may be those who do most dream most.

—Stephen Leacock

Where would we be without the dreamers of the world —the ones who took the time to balance on the edge of wonder? Amazing connections, powerful images, and creative ideas come to us in daydreams. They creep in when we least expect them, like sleek cats, then make their presence known to us with a gentle pounce.

When we give ourselves permission to daydream — to sit for a while and do nothing but be quiet with our thoughts, we give ourselves a precious gift. And who knows, we just might be giving the world a priceless gift, too! Out of the seeds of some of our dreams, great ideas will blossom.

What first step can I take today to make a dream come true?

Friends are people who help you be more yourself, more the person you are intended to be.

—Merle Shain

Sometimes a teacher, sometimes a neighbor, almost always our moms and dads encourage us to try new activities or to improve our schoolwork, sports, drawing, or gardening. Because they are our friends, they want us to be the best we can be.

Not everyone knows how to be a friend. Some people only criticize, and never praise. People who never encourage or praise us are usually unhappy with their own achievements. They don't mean us harm. Perhaps they just need a friend, too. Not only do we each need friends to help us grow, we need to be friends to others. To encourage and praise those who need it will help us in return.

Whose friend can I be today?

August 12

I don't think of all the misery, but of the beauty that still remains.
—Anne Frank

We don't find the rewards of today by searching through our misfortunes. Pausing to seek out something good for everything we find bad is a step in the right direction. We may find the good outweighs the bad.

But how much more chance we will have of living a happy day if we skip over our setbacks and concentrate as much as we can on what is going well. It is smarter to look for diamonds in a diamond mine than in a garbage dump.

Let us discard our failures, using only what we have learned from them to achieve success. Looking back at missed opportunities will make it impossible for us to recognize new chances to enjoy life to the fullest. Looking only for beauty is a beautiful thing in itself.

What beauty can I see around me right now?

*Many of our fears are tissue-paper-
thin, and a single courageous step
would carry us clear through them.*
            —Brendan Francis

There was a huge slide at the park and Jason was
afraid to go on it. There were so many steps to
climb to reach the top. All of his friends were
climbing up the steps and yelling as they came
down the long rolling slide.

"Come on," said his friend Steve. "It's lots of
fun!"

"Isn't it scary?" asked Jason.

"A little bit," answered Steve, "but you get used
to it." He ran off to go again.

Jason walked to the steps of the slide, his heart
pounding in his chest. Slowly he placed his foot on
the first step and lifted himself up. Courageously
he climbed the ladder. When he reached the high
platform he felt as if he were standing on top of the
world.

We can learn from Jason that by taking that first
step we can experience many exciting and wonderful things. We have all done it before, on the slide,
on a bicycle, in school. Why not again?

What fear can I walk through today?

August 14

> *The moment an individual can accept
> and forgive himself, even a little, is the
> moment in which he becomes to some
> degree lovable.*
>
> —*Eugene Kennedy*

If we owe a bill and pay it in full, do we return
to pay that same bill over and over again? If we
did, someone would surely question what was
wrong with us. Yet, how often do we ask forgiveness for the same thing over and over again?

How wonderful to know that we do not have to
condemn ourselves, even for not living up to a goal
we have set for ourselves. Once we say we are
sorry, we need to be willing to forgive ourselves.
After all, how else do we learn and grow except by
mistakes?

When we have forgiven ourselves, we become
free to take risks again without fear of unforgiv-
able failure, and who knows what new successes
we might attain?

Is there something I can forgive myself for today?

*Roots nourish, give us life and bind us
safely to earth. Plant them well.*
　　　　　　　　　　—Anonymous

All trees have different root systems. The pine
grows quickly, with shallow roots that spread in
every direction. A maple is a slow-growing tree,
whose roots run deeper, seeking out moisture far
into the earth. Both root systems give life, but
when the weather turns stormy and the wind
howls through the branches, the maple, with its
deeper roots, will hold fast. Though the pine
grows faster and needs only surface moisture, it
cannot withstand the storm as well.

We often want things immediately. We want to
play the piano, but only if we can learn it fast. We
want others to love us right away, or we'll give up
on them. If something we're doing doesn't go just
so right from the start, we give up.

But the permanent things in life take time to
develop. If we want our relationships, our skills,
our accomplishments, to resist the storms we all
encounter, we must allow time for them to grow
and deepen within us, and marvel, in the mean-
time, at how much we can learn from the world
around us.

What deep roots am I setting down right now?

August 16

> *I'll be the sun upon your head,*
> *The wind about your face,*
> *My love upon the path you tread,*
> *And upon your wanderings, peace.*
> —*Gordon Bok*

Today I will feel. I will feel wind and water, earth and sun. I will feel rain, the taste of it, the soft sting of its coolness. I will feel the familiar touch of my shirt against my skin, my hair across my face in the wind.

Today I will feel love like a candle on a birthday cake that never goes out, no matter how much you blow on it. I will feel compassion like a toothache, a dull pain that lets me go about my business but never goes away. I will feel joy and sorrow, pain, and pleasure. Today I will feel. I will feel like a human being, unique as a snowflake, common as grass.

How many different ways do I feel today?

The word image *is nothing more than
the French word for* picture.
— *Roseann Lloyd*

A positive image of our family can help us imagine healthy relationships. It can help us appreciate our family when it is working in a healthy way.

One woman took up looking at the pictures in her mind. At last she found one for her family, after considering ordinary pictures like a garden, a team, and a zoo. When her family is happy and thriving, she sees it as a mud pot in Yellowstone Park. Each person is energetic and relaxed. Each is free to bubble up ideas and feelings and projects, free to spout off, gurgle, and pop! Yet the family is together, sharing one old mud hole, warm and cozy, surrounded by beautiful pine trees.

Can I think of an image for my family?

August 18

> *Large streams from little fountains flow.*
>
> —*David Everett*

Somewhere nearby, no matter where we are, runs a creek. We've seen plenty of them, narrow and rocky. In summer it's hardly a creek at all, but in the spring, it feeds a mighty river.

Each of us is like that creek, a trickle contributing to some greater plan. Sometimes we feel dried up, contributing nothing. Often we feel small, rocky, not up to the task — when we can understand what the task is.

Sometimes the task seems too simple — get up each morning, love and work and live the day as honestly as we can. What kind of contribution is that? Sometimes it seems too complicated. How much more we could contribute if we could see the whole river — where it begins and ends — if we knew what would happen tomorrow.

So we ebb and flow. And in our moments of contentment, we know we are doing the best we can each day.

What contribution, however small, can I offer the world today?

A tree grown in a cave does not bear fruit.
                                    —*Kahlil Gibran*

A tree planted in a cave would soon be stopped short in its growth. There would be no room for it to grow tall or blossom. It would only grow so far and then would grow no bigger.

Fear can be like a cave. We sometimes become fearful for the same reason we might enter a cave, looking for protection. But fear protects us from the new ideas and behavior we need in order to grow. Fear can keep us huddling inside it, watching life's opportunities pass by. When fear threatens to enclose us, we can take a deep breath and begin to do what we are afraid of doing. The cave will fade away as we step out into the sun, fresh air, and storms that are a part of growing.

What fear can I overcome today?

August 20

Life can only be understood back-
wards, but it must be lived forward.
　　　　　　　—Soren Kierkegaard

Once, in a small village, there was a huge fire. The blaze spread and several homes and businesses were burned to the ground. After a long while, the fire was brought under control and put out. Villagers banded together to rebuild their town, but one quite persistent young man insisted on searching the rubble for the cause of the fire. Impatient townspeople scolded him, saying, "Why waste time searching for causes? Knowing them won't put out the blaze or repair the damage." "I know," replied the young man, "but knowing why might prevent other fires."

Sometimes we have to look at painful past experiences in order to prevent their recurrence. When we understand ourselves better, we can move beyond the past and walk towards the future with surer, safer steps.

How well can I use my past today?

Thunder is good, thunder is impressive; but it is the lightning that does the work.

—*Mark Twain*

Thunder demands our attention. From the ear-splitting boom overhead to the faint rumble in the distance, it is an impressive part of nature. Yet, it is the lightning that discharges electricity from one cloud to another, or to the earth.

We are sometimes like thunder. We may shout our intentions to family members, or quietly tell our dreams to friends. No matter how we say it, it is the ability to follow through that is most important. When we've completed what we've set out to do, we will feel a sense of satisfaction and energy. With this energy, and the knowledge we can finish what we set out to do, we will make our dreams come true.

What is left incomplete that I can finish today?

August 22

*. . .sparrow, your message is clear: it is
not too late for my singing.*
—Tess Gallagher

There was once a mother who loved to hang the laundry out on the clothesline in the back yard. Her baby crawled through the sheets and towels that almost touched the grass. The baby didn't talk yet, so nobody knew what she was thinking.

Ten years later, the baby, twelve years old, told her mother that her happiest memory of childhood was playing in her "playhouse" of laundry on the line. She remembered thinking that her mother hung the sheets out there just so she could play in the grass and wind and sun!

How wonderful to be living in a world where we can accidentally make people happy! This knowledge is a miraculous gift, and can give us reason to do every task well and with love, because it may be remembered for a lifetime by someone near to us.

What happy memory do I have of childhood?

Whenever you fall, pick something up.
                    —Oswald Avery

There was once a very active boy who fell and broke his leg. He could run again in the spring, the doctors said, but only if he stayed in bed for an entire month and kept his leg still. At first the boy fought the rule, but he found that the more he thought about things he couldn't do, the more tired and angry he felt.

His parents put in a phone by his bed and friends called every day. He'd never much liked talking on the phone, but he felt better when they called. He wrote letters and got replies, and was surprised at what fun it was. Usually, he didn't have time to write letters.

He learned to play chess and began to enjoy reading. His days were slower and quieter than he'd been used to, but he learned a month really isn't a very long time. When spring came, he was running again, a little more joyfully than before.

When we can learn to accept our troubles, we find, like the boy, that they are just packages in which new growth and discoveries are wrapped.

If something unexpected slows me down today, what joys might I find at the slower pace?

August 24

To those of us who knew the pain
of valentines that never came
and those whose names were never called
when choosing sides for basketball.
                              —Janis Ian

Each of us at some time has known the feeling of not belonging; the painful emptiness of feeling left out. We've stood on the sidelines longing to be invited into what we think is some sort of magical circle. If only they would ask us in, we think, we'd be transformed — we'd be somebody then.

But look around. The circle is composed of people just like us: insecure at times, frightened, unsure. They have felt anxiety and feared rejection just as we have.

The pain will pass, and if we use these times to get to know and understand ourselves a bit better, we'll be better able to understand others when they're feeling left out and lonely. And when it's our turn to choose a team or send a valentine, we'll remember.

Who can I remember today?

> *. . .self-love is an unequivocal accept-*
> *ance of the validity of getting what one*
> *wants — of respecting one's needs.*
> —Marion Weinstein

Once there was a woman who loved her husband and children so much that she did everything for them and nothing for herself. She thought taking care of herself was selfish. She never considered taking a vacation when she needed it. She stayed to take care of her family no matter what it cost her personally. Then she realized how much she resented them because she wasn't taking care of herself. So she began to ask for what she needed. At first, her family didn't like it. Little by little they began to notice that when she was relaxed, their lives were more serene, too. It wasn't always easy for her to love herself enough to ask for what she needed, but she learned that when she said no to demands she couldn't meet, she felt calm and centered. Best of all, she no longer resented them for asking. When she said yes, she did what they asked with real pleasure.

Do I sometimes resent doing things I could have chosen not to do?

August 26

> . . .I cannot see
> The love you offer.
> —*Emily Dickinson*

How can we make love visible; how can we give it eyes? We can make love a present, wrap it carefully as if it were a beautiful thing. We can make love a favor nobody foresaw; we can fill a cup, prepare a meal, run an errand with our love. We can make love out of real words — in a letter, a note, a simple unrhymed poem. And we can make our love visible with our eyes by making our eyes meet those of the people we love.

When we turn a feeling like love into an act, we share it with those around us, and they are encouraged to return the favor, and in this way, the world's storehouse of love increases.

How can I show the love I feel today?

*If you have butterflies in your stomach
ask them into your heart.*
                    —Cooper Edens

We've all had butterflies in our stomachs. It happens on the first day of school or the first day on a new job. It happens most anytime we try something new or risky. These butterflies are nervous and fluttery and sometimes we wish we could just go back to bed.

But the best thing we can do, and sometimes the only thing, is go right ahead and walk into that new situation with head held high. We will probably feel awkward at first, but that is natural and it will pass.

Our nervousness can change into excitement and joy for what we are doing. We can begin to feel proud when we walk through our fear. It is a true accomplishment when we don't let our fear stop us — when, instead, we let the butterfly in our hearts unfold.

When I have the butterflies today, will I enjoy their beauty?

August 28

*The route you take depends a good deal
upon where you want to go.*
　　　　　　　—*Lewis Carroll*

Day after day, the father drove to work along
the same dreary highway to the same dreary job.
Sometimes his daughter went to his office with
him. On one of these occasions she noticed a
winding road running parallel to the highway. "Oh
Daddy, let's take that road today," she suggested.
After some grumbling and mumbling, the father
agreed and turned off to take the side road.

To their delight, the road was lined with full
trees and a rainbow of flowers. They came upon a
quaint little village in which there was an office
with a sign in the window which said, "Clerk
Wanted. Inquire Within." The job seemed perfect
and the man accepted it with excitement he hadn't
felt in many years.

Sometimes we have to risk taking a different
path in order to arrive at a different place. How
else can we change things in our lives that need to
be changed? And how easy to do it, once we're
willing to risk something out of the ordinary.

What can I do that's out of the ordinary today?

*When you meet a man, you judge him
by his clothes; when you leave, you
judge him by his heart.*
> —*Russian Proverb*

The woman on the park bench was gnarled and
dirty. Her hair was an uncombed mess, her clothes
torn and old. She clutched a paper bag to her side
which seemed to contain her belongings. She sat in
the sun, humming to herself. Occasionally she
threw a bit of popcorn to ducks who waited at her
feet. A little boy and his mother sat by the lake,
not wanting to share the bench with this wild-eyed
old woman. But when the old woman beckoned to
the little boy to share her popcorn with him, he ran
to the bench and let out squeals of laughter as they
fed the hungry ducks.

Our world is full of variety and surprises.
Would we have it any other way? When we shun
someone because of the way they look, we cut
ourselves off from part of life. But when we are
ready for anything — accepting and trusting — we
are a wonder to everyone.

How shall I judge people today?

August 30

> *If I cry tears let them wash away your fears — make a rainbow of love for you.*
>
> —*Thom Klika*

It takes both sun and rain to make a rainbow in the sky. The rainbow is a rare and beautiful thing — each color brilliant beside the other. Rain falls to earth like the tears we all shed sometimes. Sunlight shines like the happiness we find inside when we feel peaceful.

The colors of the rainbow are like all the different feelings we have. Let's say red is anger and green is fear and orange is joy and violet is contentment. All these feelings create a whole person, in the same way that all these colors make the whole rainbow. We become more colorful people as we learn to express all our emotions.

A person who is learning to share feelings radiates the same kind of beauty as a rainbow in the sky.

Who can I share a feeling with today?

*I'm a trader at heart . . . except that I
don't like trades that come out equally
— that's too much like borrowing. I'd
rather trade a strong hand for a patient
ear or a story for a meal: anything that
keeps things turning over.*

　　　　　　　　　　—Gordon Bok

There is an old saying that there are just two
kinds of people in the world: givers and takers.
Those of us who are givers delight in it. We have a
buck to lend when someone is broke, a kind word
when they're down, a helping hand when they
need it. But sometimes we givers are uncomfortable when we're on the receiving end. We brush off
thanks and gifts and help, even when they're
needed or deserved.

Those of us who are takers, on the other hand,
know how to receive graciously what others have
to give; we know how to ask for what we need.
Often, however, we don't know how to give. We
may be afraid our gifts will be wrong or rejected or
laughed at.

We can all strive to become traders, people who
have learned how to both give and receive. We
each have the capacity to give what we have freely
and to ask, gratefully, for what we don't have.
That is the greatest gift of all.

What can I give and take today?

September

*Faith is the bird that feels the light when
the dawn is still dark.*
                    —*Sir Rabindranath Tagore*

In the darkness of early morning, the bird outside the window begins to sing. Soon the eastern
sky turns pink. The bird continues singing until
the first yellow rays warm its soft wings. Then it
flies away, not returning to the window until the
next morning.

We can learn from the small bird how to have
faith. We don't need to wait for something we
want before having faith we'll get it. We can begin
to show our faith by celebrating the things we usually take for granted. After all, when we take
something for granted, isn't that a selfish form of
faith? We can start by singing a song to celebrate
the new day. A day that will warm our hearts and
shed light on our actions. Like the bird's faith in
the sunrise, we need only to have faith that God
meant each day to enrich our lives.

What faith can I celebrate right now?

September 2

The answer, my friend, is blowin' in the wind, the answer is blowin' in the wind.

—*Bob Dylan*

A family is like a windchime; each member hangs in delicate balance with the others. When a problem develops for one family member, the rest of us often take on roles to try and deal with the situation. But what happens to our windchime when we're all pulling and pushing in different directions? Our balance is lost and we either all clash together or none of our chimes connect at all and there is only painful silence.

If we let go and trust in that spiritual force beyond ourselves, we discover that it is like the wind. It moves our windchime gently with a soothing breeze that allows us to relax in our places or move together as the force directs us. It brings out the beautiful harmonious notes we weren't able to produce ourselves.

How can I help us make better music together today?

Into each life some rain must fall. Some days must be dark and dreary.
—*Henry Wadsworth Longfellow*

Coping with problems and weathering troubled times is part of life. Those of us who have survived painful experiences have a duty to help younger ones prepare to face bad times by sharing the solutions we found.

When stormy weather comes, we need to feel we are like other people. It's not that misery loves company, but that we don't want to feel we're in this alone.

We will never have perfect living conditions. The only place where every day is a sunny one is in the desert. When pain comes, we can walk through our problems and settle things quickly, rather than prolonging the hurt by battling our way around the obstacles in an effort to avoid them.

What problem can I confront and eliminate today?

September 4

*Most folks are about as happy as they
make up their minds to be.*
　　　　　　　—Abraham Lincoln

Our negative thoughts can be like pebbles rolling down the mountainside. One pebble bumps into another one. The second begins rolling and slams into a third. On and on it goes until thousands of pebbles, rocks, even giant boulders are hurtling down the mountain.

When we find ourselves stuck in a rut thinking a negative thought, we can decide to stop and replace it with a positive thought. At first our single positive thought may not dislodge another one. We may have to think of several and start them rolling down the mountainside. If we practice, we will find it becomes easier for that first good thought to shake loose others. We will see our lives change when we begin to look at the positive side of things.

How can I begin to shape my outlook today?

Take care of yourself my darling
And I'll take care of me
Live your loneliness knowing
That we can both be free.
                    —Mary Lee George

Loneliness is something inside us. It's not caused by other people's behavior, though what others do may let us know we are feeling lonely. We have all experienced being alone and really enjoying it — walking by the river or singing a song we like. Feeling lonely is when we feel like nobody cares about us or wants to be with us.

Sometimes we need to give ourselves permission to feel lonely and know that we are okay no matter what we are feeling. Other times it may be wise to check with others if our feelings are true. We can ask our mother is she cares about us or ask a friend if he wants to play, and be open to the answer. When we feel lonely, we often ignore what others do or say that doesn't agree with what we believe to be true. The important thing to remember is that we are okay no matter what choice we make.

When I feel lonely, what can I do about it?

September 6

I never lose sight of the fact that just being is fun.
—*Katherine Hepburn*

The first good news each day is that we wake up. We are breathing. Our hearts are beating, our minds working. The adventure of living begins. What does the day hold in store? We have no way of knowing what surprises lie in wait for us today.

We may look forward, not just to the expected, but to the unexpected. Whom shall we meet? What will we see? What will we learn? How will we be entertained? What chances to help others will come our way? What chances to love and be loved?

Now that our eyes are opened to today's beauty, let us remain alert for new sights. Let us cry when sad, smile when touched, and laugh at what is funny in a whole new lifetime before us.

What can I be thankful for today?

*The sun's the lifegiver . . . I talk to it
like you would to a god.*
                              —*Peter Firth*

Having a power greater than ourselves to believe
in is like knowing the sun is in the sky. There are
days when the sun shines with a brilliance that
lights up everything around us — tree branches,
snowflakes, the faces of our friends. When a seed
is planted, it is the sun's warmth that invites it out
of the ground to grow into a fruit or flower. The
sun is the center the earth rotates around. The sun
gives warmth and light to the earth, sometimes in
ways we don't always notice.

There are days we do not see the sun — it is
obscured by thick clouds. Yet even on these days,
we know the sun's rays still reach the earth and
nourish her.

God nourishes and warms our lives the same
way the sun does the earth. Some days we easily
see the presence of such a power in our lives, and
other days we cannot see past the clouds. But God
gives our lives a light-filled center and nourishes us
even on quiet cloudy days.

How is God present in my life right now?

September 8

> *One must lose one's life in order to find it.*
>
> —*Anne Morrow Lindbergh*

We are often so busy trying to control the outcome of the happenings in our daily lives, so intent on projecting our tomorrows, that we let life slip by. Life is today. This is all we have for sure — the moments in our lives we cannot hold. Sometimes it feels as if those moments are beyond time and place, gifts from God to receive and give up at the same time. Like a dragonfly that lights on our hand and will either be crushed or will fly away if we try to close our fingers over it.

Life is a series of things to let go of — our friends and loved ones, our children as they grow, our dreams, or our youth. Only we ourselves, our inner selves, are a constant to be found and learned about every day, in the present moment.

How well can I enjoy each moment today?

*A terrace nine stories high begins with a
pile of earth.*

—*Lao-tzu*

Imagine yourself with a pile of dirt in front of
you and building plans for a one-story structure. It
would be easy to think, "Oh, this is impossible —
it will never get done."

But the architect hires people to help. A foundation is built, and then the frame. From there, step
by step, the rest is filled in. We have all watched a
building take shape and become a finished product.

Building plans are like the goals we all have. We
want to be a better person or friend, a better artist
or athlete. Reaching a goal is like putting up a
building. Once we have a goal, we need a strong
foundation to support us. All of us need the help
of others to reach our goals.

What small step can I take toward a goal today?

September 10

> *Give to the world the best you have*
> *and the best will come back to you.*
> *—Madeline Bridges*

Sometimes we feel lazy or bored, and then we don't do our best work. Maybe our writing becomes hard to read, or we miss a porch when delivering newspapers. Perhaps we are daydreaming instead of listening closely to what a friend is trying to tell us. When we are not really paying attention to our activities or the people around us, we'll likely miss out on something important because we do receive in equal measure what we give. And this truth works in every aspect of our lives.

When we treat our friends, our families, even people we don't know well with kindness, we'll experience kindness in return. Our own actions and attitudes toward others are what we can expect from others as well.

How can I increase the kindness in the world today?

*Good friendships are fragile things and
require as much care as any other fragile and precious things.*
—Randolph Bourne

A good friendship is like a flower garden. It
needs attention and care. We start by preparing
the soil and then planting our tiny seeds. Our
friendships have foundations like the soil, and in
them we plant seeds of trust and understanding.

Like a garden, friendships need care and love in
order to thrive. We nourish friendships with visits,
thoughtful favors, and trust. When we are feeling
down or in need of help, a friendship can offer us
more than just beauty.

When we work at our friendships, they are not
seasonal but bloom in any weather, and they surround us with comfort and the knowledge that we
have, and deserve, love.

How can I nurture a friendship today?

September 12

*No yesterdays are ever wasted for those
who give themselves today.*
—Brendan Francis

We often find ourselves yearning for tomorrow.
We get carried away thinking about the next day's
big game or camping trip. We find ourselves daydreaming about how much fun we'll have with
friends or what animals we'll see in the park.

The next day comes and perhaps the excitement
about the game diminishes because our friends
can't make it or the camping trip is cancelled because of bad weather. We feel cheated and begin
regretting the missed opportunities of yesterday.

When we find ourselves concentrating only on
tomorrow, we need to stop and look around. We'll
begin to notice the joke a friend is telling, or the
bird flying overhead. We will begin appreciating
the joys of the moment.

When we live in the moment, we have no expectations about the next moment, and without expectations, we can't be disappointed, only surprised.

What is delightful about this moment right now?

Love, a thousand, thousand voices,
From night to dawn,
from dawn to night,
Have cried the passion
  of their choices
To orb your name and keep it bright.
—*William Rose Benet*

We are each in the midst of unique lives, and our choices are based on our own experiences, so it's only natural that they all be different. One of us may choose to go to jail for protesting nuclear weapons; another may choose to pray for peace. Both are working for the same goal.

It is a sign of our love to respect others' right to choose for themselves, even to make choices we may not agree with. Perhaps a brother or sister likes music we hate, or a son or daughter wants to wear an unusual style of clothing. How often do we, in the name of love, try to force our choices on others? When we give the gift of letting loved ones choose what is right for them, it strengthens our ability to choose what is right for us.

Whose choices can I honor today, even if I disagree?

September 14

> *Something can't happen every day. You get up, go to work, come back, eat again, enjoy some leisure, go back to bed. Now that's plenty for most folks.*
> —Ntozake Shange

When we were all little kids, before we started school, the days felt so long it seemed like we had time for everything.

But when we started school, we had to start living by the clock and, in this way, we became very grown up. Sometimes we feel angry about living by the clock, all of us who are first grade and older! But there are things we can do to help us live with these limits.

First, we can learn to set a goal for each day, and once we have reached that goal — whether it's doing spelling homework, mopping the floor, or writing three business letters — we can announce to whoever happens to be around, "Now that I've completed that, I don't have to worry about one more thing to feel worthwhile."

Second, we can believe what we said! We can relax, do something fun, enjoy the pleasures that the day offers.

What is my goal for today?

*He felt frightened at being different
from his brothers and sisters. It scared
him to be different.*
                              —*E. B. White*

How ugly and wrong it makes us feel to be different: to be tall when others are short, slow when others are fast, black when others are white.

The miracle, and paradox, is that everyone is different — and that is what makes us all the same.

When we think honestly about the people we admire — friends, sports heros, actors, musicians, parents, teachers, employers — we know that all of them, as human beings, not heroes, have felt out of place in their lives, probably many times.

Believing we are alone or different cuts us off from others. Climbing over that protective wall of "differentness" is scary, but it is guaranteed to set us free.

How can I let go of my "differentness" today?

September 16

The sign must come like dawn. You cannot see its arrival, but know when it is there.

—*Diane Wakoski*

Let us take a break, sit by the river, and watch the current quietly flow. Let's just think, for a moment, about where the current is going, the shores it will brush on its way, the clouds reflected on its surface, the animals that come to drink from it, the bobbers it gently nudges downstream.

Our lives sometimes seem like the river, wandering to the west, the south, back toward the east, seemingly without direction at all. Yet we can take comfort in this thought, for, like the river, we are always headed in the direction we are meant to go. Without trying, without knowing, we are part of the larger pattern of things, and we nourish many others just by passing through their lives.

What shores will my life touch today?

Hope is the thing with feathers
that perches in the soul
And sings the tune without the words
And never stops at all.
                    —Emily Dickinson

We often hum and sing to ourselves because it makes us feel content. It is the melody itself that makes us feel good — words and thoughts do not matter.

Having hope for ourselves and for our universe is like having a melody always moving inside us. The melody may be calm or exciting, but most of all it brings with it beauty and a sense of peace. Hope can overcome the need for words and thoughts and promises. Hope is the melody that keeps us going, the hum that continues even when there are no words to the song. Hope is not a melody we think about — it just comes when we believe in the goodness of our world. If we have faith in a power greater than ourselves, we will be able to find the melody of hope inside us at all times.

What is my hope for today?

September 18

I will, I will accept myself
With hope and fear and wonder
And what I have joined together
Let no man put asunder.
                              —Dory Previn

There is a wonderful freedom in acceptance. When we accept ourselves, with all our imperfections, we can then begin to accept others just as they are. This is especially exciting when we apply this discovery to our own families. A family is like a bouquet of flowers arranged in a common vase. Each flower is different. One might be blue, one white, one a rose, one a chrysanthemum. But each adds to the beauty of the whole bouquet and enhances the vase that holds it.

It isn't important that we know why one flower is blue and one white. We don't have to understand how a rose becomes a rose to appreciate the arrangement. We just accept it for what it is. Acceptance of others does not mean agreement or approval. How boring if we only accepted those who reflected our own ideas and opinions! How dull to look upon a bouquet of exactly the same flowers.

Today, will I accept the differences between us as part of our beauty together?

*Young man, the secret of my success is
that at an early age I discovered I was
not God.*
—*Oliver Wendell Holmes*

Sometimes, in our families, we try to get parents
or brothers or sisters to treat us the way we want
them to, to do things we want them to. When
they're upset or angry with us, we try to get them
to stop, rather than allow them to be angry.

But our feelings are ours alone, and we are responsible only for how we feel. Those around us
are not the cause of our feelings. We are.

This knowledge is a big responsibility, because
we know we cannot blame others for our bad
moods. But it is a fact. And this fact is also a
wonderful freedom for us, for it means that we
also have the power to make ourselves happy, no
matter what goes on around us.

How can I make myself happy today?

September 20

> *Education should be the process of helping everyone to discover his uniqueness.*
>
> —Leo Buscaglia

We are each special, which means there is not another person just like ourselves. Nobody looks just like us. Nobody's voice sounds quite like our own. And nobody thinks through a story just like we do.

Each of us has been created for a special purpose. Maybe it's for what we'll teach a friend, or the way we'll help a sister or a brother. Every day will give us chances to offer our special talents to others. Our being alive is God's way of proving that we're important to the family, the neighborhood, the world.

What important task lies before me today?

Silently one by one,
in the infinite meadows of heaven
Blossomed the lovely stars,
the forget-me-nots of angels.
—Henry Wadsworth Longfellow

Tales told about the stars reflect a lot about the people who tell them. The constellation now called Orion was once called Hippolyta. Hippolyta was one of the Amazon queens. The Amazons were women warriors who had four leaders instead of one: two older women and two younger women. Everyone could benefit from the experience and wisdom of the older and the strength and vigor of the younger.

After Hippolyta died, they named this constellation for her to honor her and remind themselves of her wisdom and bravery.

We can draw a good lesson from the value the Amazons placed on the contribution each one could make, no matter how young or old. When we remain alert to the possibility of learning from people we hadn't seriously considered as teachers, we are reminded of our often forgotten value to others.

What can I offer in wisdom or strength to others today?

September 22

*Kindness and intelligence don't always
deliver us from the pitfalls and traps.*
—*Barbara Grizzuti Harrison*

Being human means we'll have hard times along
with pleasant ones. Whether with friends, at
school, or at home, we'll find reasons for sadness
or anger as easily as for laughter. In every part of
our lives, we're offered just what we need for
growth.

Being the best we know how to be doesn't mean
we'll escape confusion or pain. Through the troubling times we learn to trust in a Higher Power; we
learn patience; we learn to let go and let God decide outcomes. The troubling times offer us
growth and serenity, our keys to happiness.

What hidden gifts will I find in today's troubles?

*When we do the best we can, we never
know what miracle is wrought in our
life, or the life of another.*
—*Helen Keller*

It is a great loss when we underestimate the importance of our efforts in the life of another. One man, who had to spend some time in a hospital, waited day after day to receive a card or a telephone call from those who cared. Some people, who he expected to call or write, did not. Others, who the man had not felt close to, and whom he did not expect to hear from, surprised him with their concern. He came to place greater value on those who had cared enough to call or send a card.

A little act, the best we have at that moment, makes a big difference to the person on the other end. Knowing this helps us make sure that all our acts, even the smallest, are as good as we can make them, because they all make a difference.

What small acts of those around me have made a difference to me?

September 24

Notice the difference between what happens when a man says to himself, I have failed three times, and what happens when he says, I'm a failure.
—S. I. Hayakawa

What happens to us when we call ourselves names like "failure" or "dummy"? We feel we're no good and never will be. We want to stop trying because we think we'll flub up again.

But what if we begin to use different words to describe the same results? It won't change the results, but it will change us. And it will change the way we see ourselves and our actions.

Just by changing the words we use we can feel better about ourselves. Saying, "I've failed three times," means we'll try again and again and again until we succeed. It means we know God doesn't make any failures or dummies. It means God is always with us, loving us and helping us, even when trying seems difficult.

What can I change my thinking about today?

*Things don't turn up in this world until
somebody turns them up.*
　　　　　　—*James A. Garfield*

We could learn from the bears in the woods how
to turn up opportunities. To nourish themselves,
they turn over logs and stumps to get insects.
When they smell honey, they will climb a tree after
it, and when they see berries they will move
branches aside to get at them.

Like the bears, we need to turn up things for
ourselves. Perhaps we can enter a drawing or writing contest. Maybe we can try out for a team sport
or the orchestra. By doing this, we take risks
which foster our growth and build confidence, and
we turn our lives into fulfilling adventures.

Why wait for opportunity to knock when we
can knock at opportunity's door? Whatever our
interests, finding ways to enjoy them can make the
most out of the opportunities around us.

What opportunities are available to me today?

September 26

There is no hope of joy except in human relations.
— Antoine de Saint Exupery

It is hard to imagine being really joyful and excited without our family and friends. We can imagine a birthday party with no one but us attending. Even if we got many gifts, we would feel empty if there were no one around to share our excitement with.

Our joy comes from each other. Even the hard times furnish us with wonderful memories for later in life. We share the good and the bad, and the rewards of both. When our lives together seem too difficult, when it's too hard to share, too crowded to think, when there are too many disagreements, we can find comfort by looking at one another once again and seeing all the ways we are truly alike, and what we share every moment that we sometimes take for granted — our food, our thoughts, the very air we breathe.

What are the things we share right now?

Let me fly, says little birdie,
Mother, let me fly away.
            —Alfred, Lord Tennyson

Don't we all want to fly away? Isn't there a better place out there away from home? The boy can't fly, but he can climb a tree and ride the wind. The girl, high on imaginary wings, flies to her own land of dreams. Even mothers and fathers, together and alone, need to fly — away from work, house, and the everyday same old things. But we all need to return as well. We need to know that home is the one safe place to land, that there we can rest, recover our strength, tell our tales to family and friends.

Our home is safe and comfortable, but if we never leave, even for a short while, we will never take the action necessary to bring our dreams to life.

What small comfort might I give up for today in order to make a dream come true?

September 28

*One is happy as a result of one's own
efforts, tastes, a certain degree of courage, self-denial to a point, love of
work, and, above all, a clear conscience. Happiness is no vague dream,
of that I now feel certain.*

—George Sand

"We always go get a hot fudge sundae after the
school choir concert," the girl said. Her parents
laughed because their daughter said *always,* and
they had only gone to a school choir concert once.
Then the parents realized that the girl really had a
great idea.

"Yes," the mother said, "we always get a sundae
because we like to make up new traditions. We'll
have to be sure and do it tonight so we don't let the
tradition fall apart before it even gets started!"

They all laughed together and started debating
which restaurant had the best hot fudge sundae.

We all need to have special traditions with our
families. We need celebrations that have nothing to
do with official holidays. Family holidays can
mean so much more to us sometimes because they
celebrate our shared experiences in life and become
the source of happy memories for a lifetime.

What tradition can I start today?

*When people envy me I think, Oh
God, don't envy me, I have my own
pains.*
                    —*Barbra Streisand*

A forest is full of many different kinds of trees
— they are all sizes and shapes and shades of
color. It is hard to imagine a pine tree wishing it
was an oak. Or a fir tree envying the birch its
white bark. Instead, each tree catches raindrops
and reflects the sunshine in its own way.

We often find ourselves envying someone else.
We think they have more money or more friends.
We see them as better looking or luckier in some
way than we are.

It is so easy to overlook our own gifts when we
do this. We get fooled by what looks good and
forget that all human beings have some weak-
nesses and pain, just like we do. Like the trees in
the forest, we each have our own unique beauty
and talents to offer. If we believe in ourselves,
rather than envy those around us, we will grow
green and tall in our own way.

*What qualities do I have that someone might
envy?*

September 30

The house, the stars, the desert — what gives them their beauty is something that is invisible.
—Antoine de Saint Exupery

What makes our home special? Is it the shape of it, or whether or not we have carpeting? Probably not.

More likely, what make us love a place is how we feel when we are there. Home is the familiarity of pleasant smells, activities, and special people.

And when we are caught by the beauty of the stars, isn't it something that happens inside us — the breathtaking feeling of joy that is so hard to describe? The beauty of a day or a special person in our lives cannot be captured, but it can fill and warm our hearts.

Can I measure beauty today by what I feel inside?

October

Perhaps nature is our best assurance of immortality.
                          —*Eleanor Roosevelt*

Everything in nature contributes to something else — like the hundred-year-old tree that stood tall until a wind storm. The protection it gave to thousands of birds and squirrels it now gives to insects and fungi. As it slowly decays, it nourishes the ground, and from the enriched soil grow several other trees. We human beings are part of this eternal cycle, our ideas and actions enriching those around us and influencing generations yet to come. Being part of this vast plan gives us comfort, and faith that everything that happens is meant to be. Our hearts fill with joy with the knowledge that we are needed, just as every tree is needed.

How do I fit into nature's plan today?

October 2

Stars have always helped me to get things into perspective . . . I tried to let the starlight heal something deep in me that hurt.

—Madeleine L'Engle

For a long time, people have used stars to find their way in the dark. Many a lost soul has been guided by the North Star or the Big Dipper.

If we watch the sky at night, we can see thousands of twinkling stars. They are our friends. They remind us how small we are. They remind us of the vastness of the universe, of the power and beauty that surround us.

Starlight in the sky, or reflected on a lake, can comfort us when we hurt. With safe and open arms, nature accepts our sorrow, no matter how we express it. Starlight, like all of nature, reflects a light that comes from way beyond us. It is that light that heals us in a deep and quiet way.

How has nature comforted me when I am troubled?

How easy the breath that kills a flame
How hard to kindle that light again.
Cold words kill and kind words kindle,
By words withheld a dream may
   dwindle.
   —*Joan Walsh Anglund*

How we treat the people we live with affects the happiness of our family. Just as a breath can blow out a flame, a mean remark can cast a shadow across a brother or sister's heart. People of all ages have left dreams behind because no one encouraged them. They are like candles snuffed out.

On the other hand, if we see a friend or family member feeling good about something they have done, we can learn to be happy for them. If we notice their excitement and encourage them with kind and sincere words, it will help their candle burn brighter. Sharing the happiness of others will make our own candles burn brighter, and it always feels good when we receive kind words ourselves.

In what ways can I bring light and warmth with my words today?

October 4

The reason why birds can fly and we can't is simply that they have perfect faith, for to have faith is to have wings.
—*James M. Barrie*

As children, we are taught to act and think with confidence. If we have faith that something wonderful can happen, it will bring us joy. Confidence gives us the will to succeed. Without faith, we invite despair. Faith lets us win by teaming us with love and hope. When things are going well, faith encourages growth. During hard times, faith calls upon trust for added strength and inspiration. It takes such a small amount of material things to have faith. Once, a four-year-old girl found a penny and showed it proudly to a stranger. The man scoffed, "What do you expect to buy with a penny?" The child with faith replied, "I can buy a wonderful wish at a wishing well with it."

What can I have faith in today?

I think of the trees and how simply they let go, let fall the riches of a season, how without grief (it seems) they can let go and go deep into their roots for renewal and sleep.

—May Sarton

"How can I do what you say," asked the child, "and still be me?"

"Look at me," said the tree. "I bend in the wind, droop in the rain. Yet I always remain myself, a tree."

"Look at me," said the man. "I can't change."

"Look at me," said the tree. "I change every season from green to brown to green again, from bud to flower to fallen leaf. Yet I always remain myself, a tree."

"I can't love anymore," said the woman. "With my love, I have given away all that I am."

"Look at me," said the tree. "There are robins in my branches, owls in my trunk, moss and ladybugs living on my bark. They may take what I have, but not what I am."

Whether we know it or not, we are like the tree. Only our pride hangs on to a false sense of self, wanting to keep everything, refusing to follow advice or orders. What we do doesn't matter; how we do it is what counts.

What changes have I gone through without losing my real self?

October 6

*What we do upon some great occasion
will probably depend on what we already are: and what we already are will
be the result of previous years of self-
discipline.*

—*H. P. Viddon*

In the ninth inning of the baseball game with a
tie score and the bases loaded, the batter hit a
home run. The fans and the team cheered wildly,
and the batter was jubilant.

What many fans did not know was that he had
been playing on baseball teams for fifteen years.
Many times he struggled without being noticed.
He wondered if he was any good or not, and there
were days he had to make himself go out and practice. He made many mistakes, but his love and
dedication for the game had always won out.

It is the years of discipline that prepare us for
our big moments in life. Daily practice and love
give our lives a direction, even through times of
doubt and despair. By doing our best each day and
learning from our mistakes, we prepare ourselves
for the big moments — the home runs — in our
lives.

*How are my mistakes and pains today a part of my
future success?*

*There are two kinds of slaves, the pris-
oners of addiction, and the prisoners of
envy.*

—*Ivan Ilich*

No emotion brings us more personal pain or
wastes more of our time than envy. When we envy,
we are never free from stress, because envy takes
no holidays. Shakespeare called envy the green
sickness. Envy magnifies molehills into mountains.

Just how foolish envy truly is becomes clear
when we think of it as a row of hooks on which to
hang grudges. When we envy others, especially
our family members, we blind ourselves to the
good we could see in all people. We are ignoring
life's flowers to gather bouquets of weeds.

When we envy the accomplishments or possessions of another, we will be better off if we look to
our own prized possessions, to those things in ourselves that no one else has in exactly the same way.

What riches do I have within and around me?

October 8

Learn what you are and be such.
—Pindar

The most precious gift we can give those closest to us is honesty. Yet we often hide our true selves from friends, fearing we won't be accepted or loved if we let them see the real us. Often, we show parts of ourselves that hide who we really are. We have often heard ourselves or others say, "My parents would just die if. . .," or, "don't argue in front of the children."

If we hide too much behind false images, we run the risk of losing track of what is real and what is false. We become actors instead of real people, trying to please Aunt Jane, our grandparents, our big brother, or our children.

When we conquer our fear of letting others in, we are able to see ourselves honestly. When we discover that others accept us as we are, we can accept and love ourselves. To know oneself is to know a person of value.

What part of me have I been hiding?

> *. . .but time and chance happeneth to
> them all.*
>
> —*Ecclesiastes*

Life, director of the comedy, always lets things
get a little out of hand. We all know what would
be normal and right, but the right horse sometimes
finishes last in the race, and the jerk has all the
money. The wise people, like us, are ignored by
all, and the good woman gets in trouble with the
law. The saint cheats on his income tax, but he
never gets caught the way the needy ones like us
do, and the worst sinners get saved in the nick of
time, while the fittest sometimes just drop dead.

If all the best laid plans go wrong, maybe we are
meant to learn that such important things aren't so
important, after, all.

If the skies are custard pies waiting to plop down
on our hopeful faces, maybe it is best to accept the
gift, count it a blessing, and lick our chops.

How have my failures been successes in disguise?

October 10

> *Look, the wind vane fluttering in the*
> *autumn breeze*
> *Takes hold of certain things that*
> *cannot be held.*
>
> — *Feng Chih*

When we think we are losing our grip, we have good reason to look up. Consider the moon suspended in the sky, how it continues to come and go, follows its natural law, and never really loses face. Consider the sun, the stars, the seasons, how they refuse to abandon us, to let go of their hold on our lives. And come closer to home. We can marvel at the magic of small efficient things — the toaster and stove, the light in the room, the words in a good book that are permanent, faithful, and clear. We can consider how music, without saying a word, still speaks to us, and how a few friends, maybe miles away, continue to hang on to the strength of our small and faithful words.

We can keep in mind that we are part of a complex and loving system, and our grip can never be lost.

How do I see my unity with my surroundings today?

A musician must make music, an artist must paint, a poet must write, if he is to be at peace with himself. What a man can be, he must be.
                              —*Abraham Maslow*

The same is true of a seamstress, carpenter, homemaker, lawyer, or mechanic. The question is, Who and what am I? What must I do to be at peace with myself? What can I be, for that is what I must be?

A lucky few of us find the answers to these questions fairly early in life, and we work to develop into the people we can be and must be. We do that by looking at our deepest desires, and ask what would bring fulfillment for us. We ask what we would enjoy doing most, what we believe we have the ability to be really good at. What is it that sometimes burns within us to be expressed or done? The answers to what we can be, what we must be, come from within, through asking ourselves these questions.

What kind of a person am I capable of being?

October 12

We can secure other people's approval,
if we do right and try hard; but our
own is worth a hundred of it. . . .
        —Mark Twain

There was once a young girl who thought that if only she tried a little harder, she could please her parents; if only she were prettier her friends would like her better. She tried constantly to gain their approval. Sometimes they said they liked her and sometimes they didn't.

Then one night a fairy came to her in a dream and told her, "You are fine just the way you are. You don't have to change. I want you to start noticing your own beauty and loving yourself exactly the way you are."

Doing what the fairy suggested — giving love and approval to herself — wasn't easy, but she found that when she did it she felt a peace that was not dependent on what others thought. She thanked her fairy for caring enough to come and give her such wise advice.

What are some things I like about myself?

*. . .(the king) can deprive them of the
benefit of sun and rain,. . .and they are
at the same time pelted from above
with great stones,. . .while the roofs of
their houses are beaten to pieces.*
— *Jonathan Swift*

How do we punish those momentarily gone
wrong? Do we try hurting with words — jab them
in the heart with some spear-shaped phrases, slap
them in the face with an insult or two? Maybe we
like to poison them with a strong dose of silence.
Have we tried to make them feel bad by making
them feel sorry for us? Do we remind them daily
that what went wrong with our lives is really all
their fault?

We must remember that we are the rulers of our
own lives only, and this knowledge gives us the
power to punish only ourselves. It also gives us
control over our lives, so that others' actions need
not wrong us, and we need not punish.

Have I been punishing someone?

October 14

If you're never scared or embarrassed or hurt, it means you never take any chances.

—Julia Soul

Do we avoid making new friends because we're scared they won't like us? Do we get embarrassed when we make a mistake and avoid trying again? When we get our feelings hurt, do we think we're bad, or that something is wrong with us?

Being scared or shy or hurt are all part of being alive. When we try to stay away from painful feelings, we keep ourselves from having many wonderful adventures. If we're afraid to meet new people, we may never have any close friends. If we stop trying when we're embarrassed, we may never learn a better way of doing things. And if we don't share our hurt feelings, we may never find out that everyone else has the same feelings we have.

What can I try again today that I failed at yesterday?

. . .ere it vanishes
Over the margin
After it, follow it,
Follow The Gleam.
                    —Alfred, Lord Tennyson

It is difficult to find words for the "Gleam" we pursue. What it is, we are never too sure. We see it best in our daily dreams, while we're staring out a window at nothing at all. Sometimes it appears between the words in a book; it is always sure to be there when we sit alone to write down our own thoughts. We see it in the autumn woods, feel its heavy breathing in ocean waves. It is suddenly a skylark in flight, a falling leaf, a flower we have reluctantly picked. It makes us feel sad but good. It is always luring us on, always beautiful.

Is it love? Success? Peace? It may be any or all of these things, and we may find it through another person, or some talent we have, or a thing of beauty we stumble upon. And it is there within us, always, waiting to be found.

In what ways can I follow the Gleam I see in my life today?

October 16

> *Therefore do not be anxious about to-
> morrow, for tomorrow will be anxious
> for itself.*
>
> —*Matthew 6:34*

To worry about something ahead of time is a waste of time and energy that could be better spent on living a full life today.

For instance, if we spend hours today worrying about an important test at school tomorrow, we can't very well concentrate on studying. And if we lie awake tonight agonizing over what we don't know or haven't studied, we're going to be exhausted tomorrow when we take the test.

Wouldn't it be much better to focus on doing all we can today to prepare for the test, and then, knowing we've done our best, let go of it tonight and get a good night's sleep? In fact, if we do that every day of the year, when a big test comes along, we'll know we're as ready as we can be, and won't have a thing to worry about. What a relief it is to know we've done our best today and every day.

What can I do well today so I won't worry about it tomorrow?

Fear makes strangers of people who should be friends.
   —Shirley MacLaine

No one is brave every moment; each of us feels awkward, shy, perhaps even ugly or dumb part of the time. If we could understand that about each other, it would make it easier for us to be friendly and willing to talk to someone new. Instead, we often sit back, waiting to be noticed; waiting for someone to invite us to join in an activity.

We are all so much alike, yet we are so certain we're different. Being self-conscious is normal. Even those who are the most popular suffer the same fears as the rest of us. The better we understand the ways we are the same, the easier it will be to make friends with someone new. And it's through friends that we grow and are strengthened for whatever lies ahead.

What new person can I offer friendship to today?

October 18

One will rarely err if extreme actions be ascribed to vanity, ordinary actions to habit, and mean actions to fear.
—*Friedrich Nietzsche*

Sometimes we begin to believe someone close to us is being mean deliberately. This may happen when a good friend suddenly stops inviting us to her house. She may be scared to have others over because her parents are having problems, or for some other reason that has nothing to do with us.

But we often fear that it is because of something we said or did. We find ourselves becoming scared and pulling away. If we ask for God's help in turning our fear around, we can overcome it and ask our friend why she stopped inviting us over. Most times we will find that our friend had no idea her actions affected us the way they did. We can then laugh at ourselves for our fears and applaud ourselves for overcoming them.

What treasure might I find beneath my fear today?

*All power is a trust. We are account-
able for its exercise. From people and
for people all power springs, and all
must exist.*
—*Benjamin Disraeli*

The sun is power. It warms, it burns, it feeds the
plants without which we could not live. Yet, for all
its power, the sun cannot make so much as a rainbow by itself. For that, it needs the rain, at just the
right time and angle.

No matter how strong we are — or smart or
talented or attractive — we realize our full power
only by filtering it through others. Our most
meaningful achievements are born of combined efforts. Even when we do something that feels like
ours alone — paint a painting, win an award, hit a
home run — there is always a constellation of
friends and family and teachers, even enemies,
who've been a part of our success.

Like the rain's part in the rainbow, the contribu-
tions of others do not detract from our achievements, but enhance them and bring them to their
fullest light.

How are others enhancing my growth today?

October 20

> *The bough which has been downward thrust by force of strength to bend its top to earth, so soon as the pressing hand is gone, looks up again straight to the sky above.*
>
> —*Boethius*

When we are down, low, depressed, why can't we ignore the desire to rise up again? Because we're like plants that need pure air, water, and sun. Because no matter how bent and old, we just keep wanting to grow up. Because there is a natural spring in us like that which makes flowers leap from the earth in May. Because we have hidden wings. And if we listen, we can feel the difference between wrong and right: we know the difference even with our eyes closed. Therefore we should not try putting ourselves down, for we will spring up again, sure as Spring.

What is the main way I try to put myself down?

Great events make me quiet and calm;
it is only trifles that irritate my nerves.
—Queen Victoria

Isn't that always the way? We cope with major events, like births and weddings, fairly well. It is the little things — so inconsequential in the long run — that upset us. If the kids don't pick up their rooms, or dinner is late, or we can't go to the movies because we haven't done our homework, we become irritated and annoyed. Minor things like these upset us much more than they should.

Are they really so important? A messy room is not a terminal illness. A late dinner won't effect our health unless we get so upset about it we make ourselves sick. We'll survive.

If we think back to the last time we were angry or upset, does it seem important now? We probably can't even remember why we reacted that way. How much better life is when we let go of the little irritations.

What irritation can I let go of today?

October 22

Sometimes it takes a rainy day just to let you know, everything's gonna be alright.

—*Cris Williamson*

Rainy days let us slow down. We are busy people, driving ourselves to go places and get things done. But rain seems to slow life down, even in our hearts. And slowing down can show us the peace in our lives, the peace of knowing we have all we need right inside us. The pressures of the world can drop away for a time while we reflect.

As the rain soaks into the ground, its serenity enters our hearts. Leaves on trees begin to look more green. Plants and flowers are no longer thirsty. When we slow down, we can be comforted by what we have in our hearts, knowing everything is going to be all right.

What comfort can I find within myself right now?

I never saw a wild thing sorry for itself.
—D. H. Lawrence

Sometimes when we feel sorry for ourselves we will sit alone in our bedroom. We may even feel so down in the dumps that we decide to stay there, indulging in self-pity, thinking about how the world is against us.

However, if we use our imagination to step outside our own point of view for a moment, we might think differently. If we were deer in the forest, we would be thinking about keeping safe from the wolves, and where our next meal would be coming from.

The animals have no time to feel sorry for themselves, they are too busy doing what has to be done to survive, and each thing that happens presents a new survival problem to be solved.

When we feel blue, it helps to keep this in mind. If we have the time to feel down, and can get physically comfortable while doing it, how bad can the problem really be?

In what ways is my life comfortable, easy, and full of love?

October 24

Before he closed his eyes, he let them wander round his old room. . .familiar and friendly things. . .which were so glad to see him again and could always be counted on for the same simple welcome.

—Kenneth Grahame

When they moved into the house, the room at the top of the stairs was just a junk room. As the years passed, they slowly transformed the room into a guest room.

When they decided they needed another voice in the house, they transformed the room again: out went the fold-out couch, in came a crib and rocking chair; off went the art gallery prints from the walls, up went Winnie the Pooh. It was no longer a guest room, but a place for the baby, a new — and permanent — member of the family.

We always have room for more in our lives. When we are ready for it, what we need for growth will emerge.

What do the rooms inside our homes and ourselves have to tell us about the way we live our lives?

I love him and I cannot seem to find him.

—Ovid

Where can we find the ones we love? Do they always live in our world, or do we have to go out of our way? They often are not at home; we can find them at their work. Their play is different from ours; we could try having their kind of fun.

Too often, we look only for friends who are much like ourselves, and we tend to avoid those who are not. This kind of narrow-mindedness isn't fair to ourselves or others. We are each unique, like the pieces of a puzzle. We are each necessary to the whole picture.

When we go out of our way to know someone else better, we stretch our own boundaries, we give ourselves new space in which to grow.

What part of my life can I discover in someone new today?

October 26

Whoever is happy will make others happy, too.
—Anne Frank

Anne Frank had good reason to be unhappy, full of fear, and deeply discouraged. Years of her life were spent in a small apartment hiding from the Nazis who wanted to destroy her and her family. Yet even in this little hiding place she had happiness. It was something she had inside which did not depend on what happened around her. She had riches of the heart. She had faith that kept her going. She had love and concern for her family and others which made even a restricted life very rich with feelings. It is tempting to believe that we will be happy when we have something outside ourselves which will make us happy. But happiness is not something we have to find outside; the seeds are in our hearts already.

What happiness can I find in my latest setback?

Walk. Don't walk.

—Traffic Light

Signs direct us on our way in life. Traffic lights tell us to walk (or not), Golden Arches point us to dinner, geese flying south herald the coming winter, flashing neon tells us what to buy. We know how to read these signs of worlds and weather; they help to guide us on our journey.

We can learn to read the signs of human beings, too, to be detectives of the human spirit. Laugh lines around eyes and mouth, the texture of hands, tension in jaws and shoulders can tell much about a person, if we stop to look. All around us are signs that tell us others feel the pain and joy we feel, others need us as we need them, we are understood, and we are not alone.

The marvelous bonus in learning to read these signs in others is that we can begin to let ourselves be read, also.

Will I make good reading for others today?

October 28

I feel no need for any other faith than
my faith in human beings.
                        —*Pearl S. Buck*

We owe each other respect. We cannot expect to be respected if we don't respect others around us. When we respect others, we respect their property and personal belongings as well as their self-esteem and their right to voice an opinion. Respect is a way of cooperating with each other.

We can imagine a submarine where crew members did not respect each other's personal belongings or their ability to do the job. The ship would soon stop functioning because of the chaos. In a family we live in close quarters, like a submarine crew. Respect for each other is one of the things which keeps chaos from breaking out. When we grow in respect for each other's property, abilities, and self-esteem, we soon see how valuable each member of our crew really is.

How can I show respect to those around me today?

*There is nothing so moving — not even
acts of love or hate — as the discovery
that one is not alone.*

—Robert Ardrey

Our fears are normal. Some of us fear going to a
new school and making new friends. Taking an
important test causes jitters in the bravest looking
person. Maybe staying alone in the house for the
first time has you looking under beds and in
closets every time you hear a strange noise. Our
fears are merely reminders that we've forgotten to
let God help us out.

So often we think we're alone, but we never are.
We each have a Higher Power just waiting to be
relied on. Nothing is too difficult or fearful for us
to handle with the help of our Higher Power.
When we develop the habit of letting God ease our
way, our fears are gone.

*Today, which fear can I replace with trust in my
Higher Power?*

October 30

You have three choices: keep on fight-
ing, ignore each other, or make up and
be friends.

          —John Knoblauch

Once there were four sixth-graders — two boys and two girls — who started to fight even though they'd been friends for years. One morning at the bus stop, the boys started playing keep-away with the girls' shoes and wouldn't give them back. One of the mothers called the school.

Later that day, the counselor called them in and asked them what the fight was all about. They said they didn't really know.

"Well," said the counselor, "it doesn't really matter why you started fighting. Right now, you've got three choices: keep on fighting, ignore each other, or make up."

The group chose to ignore each other, after discussing it among themselves. They were happy to be able to stop fighting. About the time of winter vacation, they decided to be friends again.

What conflicts can I resolve by letting them be?

*The only sense that is common in the
long run is the sense of change — and
we all instinctively avoid it.*
              —E. B. White

Nature reveals to us a world that is always
changing. No two sunsets are alike. Winter brings
invigorating days while spring brings new buds
and blossoms every day. Summer brings lazy
warmth and star-filled evenings while fall brings
crisp afternoons and a sense of nostalgia.

Even though nature shows us a constantly
changing world, we often resist the changes in our
own lives. Changes can be both hard and sad, yet
they are a part of life. Perhaps we are moving on to
a new school or a new neighborhood, or perhaps
we are feeling the changes that come with a di-
vorce in the family.

With every change we say a sad goodbye to
something old, something familiar — in the same
way we feel sadness for summer's end when the
first leaves begin to fall. Yet every change also offers us the excitement and potential of a new season — with its own opportunity for new smells,
special gifts, and invigorating days.

How have I changed today?

November

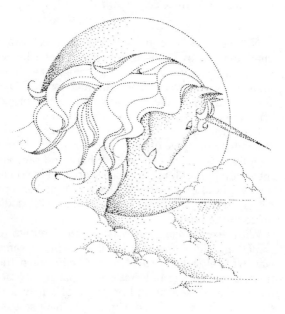

Oh, this is the creature that doesn't exist. . . .In fact, it never was. But since they loved it, a pure beast came to be.
—*Rainer Maria Rilke*

The unicorn, serene and white, is a strong and graceful animal with the body of a horse. A single white horn grows from its brow, making it unique among all animals. It is gentle, shy, and good, and though stories have been told about it for centuries, many people say it never existed. We call it a myth, yet in telling its story, we make it real.

Friendship is like the unicorn: created from faith. Before we speak, reach out, believe in the possibility of relations with another, friendship does not exist. But when we share a meal, a joke, or a walk — a piece of ourselves — we open up to two friends . . . one in the other person, the other within ourselves.

How does sharing myself with another create a friend within me?

November 2

For no actual process happens twice;
only we meet the same sort of occasion
again.

—*Suzanne K. Langer*

Today is not going to be like yesterday. Nor will it resemble tomorrow. Each day is special and promises us many new ideas — perhaps the chance to make a friend, or to learn something interesting from a teacher or a book. Some activities today will be familiar, just like playing a game for the second, third, or tenth time is familiar. And yet, the way each player moves the pieces around the board will be different. The excitement about today is that it is full of surprises. Every thing we do, every conversation we have, will not be repeated in just the same way again, and this reminds us how special each of us is.

What new discovery will I make today?

Here's Sulky Sue
What shall we do?
Turn her face to the wall. . . .
                    —Mother Goose

When she put her Sulky Sue up against the wall, was this mother a wise or silly goose? If Sue was confused, could she talk sense with a wall? If she was angry, would the wall ever know why? If she was sad, would the wall wipe her tears away? If she was lonely, would the wall take her by the hand? Some walls are built for support, others to keep people away. To sulk is to look for support, someone strong to hold us up, not a silly goose who will turn us away.

Sulking is not the best way to look for help, and when we sulk, we are likely to end up isolating ourselves in some corner of our own making. And on the other hand, when we see another sulking, how much better it is to offer support instead of isolation!

Do I build walls of isolation, or walls of support?

November 4

> *Being entirely honest with oneself is a good exercise.*
>
> —*Sigmund Freud*

The truth is our friend. It is a rough and humble kind of friend — but a friend nonetheless. Each of us will need to learn to spend time with this friend because it is one that is not easy to escape. It is always turning up when we least expect it. The truth about ourselves is hard to avoid. It seems to knock at our door until we let it in.

Perhaps we have played the game of hide and seek sometime in our lives. Sometimes we tell little lies about ourselves to impress others, or we act in ways that, deep down, we know are not really the way we want to be. We can never be comfortable this way. We know what it is like to hide and try to keep from being found. The truth about us is an expert player. It seeks us out until we put our arms around it and welcome it.

Is there something I am hiding from today?

*Nature, the Gentlest Mother, is
Impatient of no Child. . . .*
              —Emily Dickinson

When a girl sits on the seashore, the waves do not try to slap her around. When a boy wanders alone in a field, the sky does not accuse him of talking back. When a man is alone in the woods, does the earth nag him for failing once more? And when a woman is alone in the park, does the wind whisper behind her back? Nature never blames or condemns: she gives us freedom of thought and plenty of space. Nature's ways are proven and true; she lets us grow at our own rate. Nature brings us sleep, dawn, new days; she is full of new life.

We are a part of nature, and everything we do is part of it. We can find comfort in this knowledge, if we take the time to remember it when we are feeling bad. Nature is always willing to share its serenity.

When we escape to nature, what feelings do we have that we want to take back home with us?

November 6

Work is love made visible.
            —*Kahlil Gibran*

Family members show love and concern for others through their work. Parents might build a bookcase or prepare the meals. Children might help by emptying the wastebaskets. All are showing love through what they do. In our lives together, our work is an important way of saying I love you. We will still want to say those words to family members. We will still want to give them lots of hugs and kisses. But our work shows how much we care, and who is important to us. Our work around the house is an investment. It makes a home for all of us, constructed of visible love.

How can I make our home a better one today?

*I never found the companion that was
so companionable as solitude.*
        —Henry David Thoreau

One of the greatest gifts of our lives is the ability
to enjoy solitude. Many of us are unable to enjoy
this gift. We are too busy — busy with work, with
friends, with entertainment.

When we slow down, we find out we can feel
peaceful when we are alone. For most of us, solitude is ordinary — we each find our private place
and take up our favorite activities: fishing, sewing,
writing, building models, making pictures. These
simple activities are so much fun it's hard to figure
out why it took us so long to calm down and enjoy
them.

Our dreams may be quite ordinary. We can
learn how to find them.

*What ordinary activities have I been putting off
because I think I'm too busy?*

November 8

*All acts performed in the world begin
in the imagination.*
—*Barbara Grizzuti Harrison*

We use our imaginations to plan how we're going to build a model car or plane, rearrange the furniture in our rooms, even dress for a special party. The imagination is like a big piece of drawing paper on which we sketch the way we want something to look.

When we don't know just how to begin a task, the imagination gets us started. It's like having the directions for playing a new game. Dreams about the future, where we want to go, the jobs we want to have, are made more real when we "draw" them in our minds. The imagination gives us courage, too.

Do I have the courage today to imagine a better me?

Love is something if you give away,
you end up having more.
—Malvina Reynolds

The other side of giving is taking. Many of us were brought up to believe that it's not okay to take, so we diminish admiration that people give us. "Oh, this old rag, I got it at a garage sale for next to nothing." This response to a compliment can take away the joy of giving it from the person who admired the way we looked.

Giving needs taking to complete it. We can keep the cycle of generosity going by taking gracefully. A world without those who take would be unbalanced. When someone gives us love, appreciation, or a gift, we can show our real pleasure with a simple thank you, and stop thinking we don't deserve it.

Can I accept what's given to me today in the spirit it's offered?

November 10

He who has courage and faith will never perish in misery!
—*Anne Frank*

Someone once said happiness is like a butterfly: if we chase it, we'll never find it. But if we sit quietly, it will come and land on us. Faith and courage are the same. All we have to do is sit quietly and ask for these gifts from God. In time, and with patience, they will be ours, and so will the happiness we can then pass on to others.

Anne Frank wrote the above words facing a concentration camp and certain death. If she could find happiness and faith and courage within herself under those circumstances, then certainly we can too. These gifts are ours, already within us, if we but look for them.

What can I ask for today?

We shall not cease from exploration,
And the end of all our exploring
Will be to arrive from where we started
And know the place for the first time.
—T. S. Eliot

We spend much of our lives looking forward to milestones we hope will mark our passage into wisdom — that time and place when once and for all we will know all there is to know.

When I am thirteen, I'll be grown up, we say. When I am sixteen, eighteen, 21, drive a car, graduate, marry, write a book, own a house, find a job, or retire; *then* I'll be grown up.

When we seek complete transformation, mere insight is disappointing. We find we don't know all there is to know — not at thirteen or 35 or 80. We are still growing up.

The baby, the child, the younger person each of us was yesterday is still with us; we continue to love, hate, hurt, grieve, startle, delight, feel.

There is no magic moment of lasting enlightenment, simply a series of fleeting moments lived one at a time each day. They bring us home to who we've always been.

What small thing have I learned today?

November 12

*No life is so hard that you can't make it
easier by the way you take it.*
— *Ellen Glasgow*

Jimmy and Karen were out catching insects for
their science class. Jimmy had caught a gray moth
and Karen a monarch butterfly.

"My moth sure isn't very pretty," Jimmy said as
he looked at the two insects. "Now I'll have to
catch something else."

"Oh, but it is," said Karen. "See what a fat body
your moth has compared to my butterfly, and it's
got fuzzies on its wings."

"You're right," said Jimmy, beginning to smile at
his moth. "I was almost going to let him go."

How many times in the past have we taken just a
quick look at something before rejecting it? Often,
simply because a thing isn't quite what we expected, we don't give ourselves a chance to discover what it is that makes that thing beautiful.
There is a secret beauty in everything, even ourselves. When we take the time to seek it out in
other people and things, especially those that have
disappointed us, that beauty is reflected in us, too.

*Can I find the beauty in something common to-
day?*

*The measure of a man's real character is
what he would do if he knew he could
never be found out.*
                        —Thomas Macaulay

Remember the tale about the poor, tired shoemaker who cut out his last bit of leather and
awoke to find a beautiful pair of shoes sewn for
him? Night after night two little elves secretly
worked from midnight to dawn sewing shoes to
help the old craftsman. Helping the shoemaker
without his knowing who they were made the
elves very happy, and they danced and sang as
they worked away. These elves knew their reward
was in the doing of the good deed, not in the discovery of them doing it.

What secret gift of kindness can I give today?

November 14

People are lonely because they build walls instead of bridges.
—Joseph Fort Newton

Communication is much more than words. Words are merely fingers pointing the direction to understanding — they are not understanding itself. To really communicate with someone, we have to allow ourselves, just for a moment, to become that other person. When we do this, we begin to be able to see beyond the masks that hide what another person is really feeling.

When we take the time to really see others, we may discover they are frightened, timid people longing for understanding. When we get beyond reacting to their outward behavior and move toward viewing their inner selves, it is much easier to extend a hand of friendship, to say we care, and truly mean it.

Who can I see as they really are today?

Growing is like running a twenty-six mile marathon. If we give up on the twenty-fourth mile, we will never know what it feels like to finish the race.

—Anonymous

There will be times in our growth when we will want to give up. Our pain seems to have no end to it. In a sense, we are like the runner of a marathon on her twenty-fourth mile. She may think she cannot finish the race; she may lose her ability to see things as they are.

If she can remember previous successes, she will no doubt make the decision to go on, to at least give the race her best shot. It does not matter how many people come in before or after her. It matters only that she has not given up. When she crosses the finish line, the pain turns quickly into joy.

When we refuse to give up, we give ourselves an accomplishment we can rejoice in, the reward of knowing we have done our best.

What can I finish that I gave up on earlier?

November 16

> *One is forever throwing away sub-
> stance for shadows.*
> —Jennie Jerome Churchill

Sometimes we trade possessions with our friends. Maybe we want to add to our collection, or perhaps we just do it to get someone to like us. But if we try to buy friendship, we'll be sad later when we realize we've lost a prized possession and not gained a friend.

Our friendships come when we least expect them, often with people who have something in common with us. They will not be friendships we have to buy, but relationships to treasure and have for years. These friendships will teach us to respect ourselves and our friends.

Am I making good friends, or bad trades?

Down in a green and shady bed
A modest violet grew;
Its stalk was bent, it hung its head,
As if to hide from view.

—Jane Taylor

Shyness can be painful. Those of us who are shy do not choose to be this way. There are no quick and easy solutions to shyness, but it isn't the worst thing that could happen to us. And there are some things we can do about it. We can be willing to talk about it with someone we trust. We can exercise to build strength and self-confidence, and we can avoid dwelling on the problem. Most of all, we should not let shyness keep us from doing things. We may be a little uncomfortable, but that doesn't have to stop us from doing the task at hand to the best of our ability.

We can be assured that the ability to succeed is within us, and keep in mind that, if we offer love to those around us, their answering love will help us overcome our shyness.

What am I no longer too shy to try today?

November 18

> *One comes in the end to realize that there is no permanent pure relationship and there should not be.*
> —Anne Morrow Lindbergh

Whether we are teenagers in love for the first time, or parents who have been married for twenty years, relationships can turn into obsessions if we're not careful. We can lose our sense of self and only feel complete when we're with the other person. We can become totally attached and dependent on the primary person in our lives for all our needs.

We need to remember that we can be a good partner in a relationship only if we feel complete within ourselves. Keeping ourselves open to change in our surroundings, our loved ones, and especially ourselves helps us stay whole.

We learn, first, to be ourselves, to make independent choices. We dare to do things on our own. Things as simple as going for a walk by ourselves and smelling the scents of nature. Being ourselves means bringing our own world to meet the world of our loved ones, rather than depending on them to make our world.

Am I making my own happiness so I may share it with others?

*We all fear what we don't know — it's
natural.*
                            —Leo Buscaglia

If we put a blindfold over our eyes and begin to
walk around an open field, we would feel unsure
with each step. We might be afraid of falling,
afraid of walking over some unseen edge and hurting ourselves.

When any of us face something and we don't
know what the outcome will be, we often feel
blindfolded. We fear we may get hurt. We fear we
can't do it. We have a hard time trusting ourselves.
A blind person often finds help or guidance from
others, or will gain confidence by walking on —
slowly at first, finding trust and sureness with each
step.

These same things help us when we are afraid. It
is also helpful to remember there is no right or
wrong way to explore what faces us — only our
own way.

What new trust can I place in myself today?

November 20

*Without solitude, there can be no real
people.*

—John Euder

We all need some time alone. It's a good idea to
set aside a few minutes every day to be alone with
ourselves. This is a very special time that is all our
own. It's a time to relax and refresh ourselves.

This goes for every member of the family, and
it's important that we allow others some time for
themselves. It shows them we respect, love, and
care about them. Without that solitude, they cannot be truly themselves — and neither can we.

Nature teaches us that each thing, even the earth
itself, needs a retreat. Bears hibernate; cats crawl
off out of sight, even the plants disappear for the
winter. It is this time that refreshes life for the
Spring to come. If we want to have healthy, fulfilling relationships with each other, we all need time
to ourselves every day. Without being "real people" — truly ourselves — how can we be full members of our family?

How can I better spend my time alone today?

*We decided that it was no good asking
what is the meaning of life, because life
isn't an answer, life is the question, and
you, yourself, are the answer.*
—Ursula K. LeGuin

How many times have we felt like we were drift-
ing aimlessly, constantly searching for meaning in
a world that seems so mixed up, seeking direction
but getting nowhere? But looked at differently,
"nowhere" becomes "now here." When we take
things apart, stand back, and examine them from
a different angle, we often find we held the answer
from the beginning. Sometimes, when we're con-
vinced we are the problem, we discover we were
the solution all along.

When we look for true understanding, we can
be sure it exists in this moment, and that we can
find it within ourselves, with God's help.

What question do I seek an answer to today?

November 22

The greater part of our happiness or misery depends on our dispositions and not on our circumstances.
—Martha Washington

We all have friends who seem happy even though they run into lots of bad luck. And we all know other people who seem grumpy all the time. Nothing makes them very happy. It's puzzling, but some people have decided, maybe without even knowing it, that life is fun and should be enjoyed. No bit of bad luck has to make us miserable unless we let it.

A broken bike, a lost math assignment, a rained out picnic are things that might make us miserable. But we can decide they won't. Feeling happy can be a habit — just like brushing teeth before bedtime.

Will I stop and think today before I let things make me unhappy?

*Happiness is not a place to travel to. It's
a way of getting there.*
— *Anonymous*

Those of us who climb mountains find joy in
reaching the top. However, the climb would not
make much sense if there were not things to enjoy
on the way up. If we groan and complain, it will be
hard to feel joy at the summit. However, if we are
able to enjoy each day's journey, it makes all the
difference in the world. In the midst of each chore,
we can notice the sunset or the unique and beautiful surroundings of each day.

Each of our days is different. Happiness is not a
goal we are struggling to reach some time in the
future. It is a gift we can give ourselves today. If we
enjoy some parts of each day of our hike, we will
also feel joy at the summit.

What form will my gift of happiness take today?

November 24

> *I went to sleep with gum in my mouth
> and now there's gum in my hair and
> when I got out of bed this morning I
> tripped on the skateboard and by mis-
> take I dropped my sweater in the sink
> while the water was running and I
> could tell it was going to be a terrible,
> horrible, no good, very bad day.*
> —Judith Viorst

Some days, for all our good intentions, seem to go sour from the start. Maybe we're tired or feeling ill or preoccupied with a problem that seems insurmountable. Maybe we just got up on the wrong side of the bed.

Living one day at a time means getting the most we can out of today. It also means we know today does not have to doom or dictate tomorrow. If we have a bad day today, that's all it is — a bad day. It does not mean we're bad or that the world is against us or that we might as well give in to our worst attitudes and behaviors since nothing is going right anyway. And it does not mean tomorrow will be a bad day, too.

When we have a bad day — and everyone does — there are a few things we can do while we wait it out. We can slow down. We can be quiet. We can pray. And we can let go. How else will we be able to recognize a wonderful day?

Am I living today — good or bad — and not tomorrow or yesterday?

*All music is what awakes from you
when you are reminded by the instruments.*

—*Walt Whitman*

A small group of friends sat in a room around a
record player. It was a heavy old thing, with parts
that had to be operated by hand and only one
speaker — nothing like a modern stereo at all, but
more like an antique phonograph. The record — a
recording of their favorite music — was old, too,
and scratched, its grooves worn smooth as a stone
in some places. The tone arm skipped and
scratched, and the sound was tinny, hard on the
ears.

Most of the friends squirmed in their seats as
they listened, and several grumbled that it was impossible to hear the music with such inferior
equipment.

But one of the group sat listening, her eyes
closed, swaying to the music and humming softly
to herself.

"How can you enjoy this?" the others asked.

"Ah," she said with a mysterious smile. "I am
listening beyond the recording to the music I know
is there!"

Can I find the music that's playing for me today?

November 26

*Giving up is not giving in, nor is it fail-
ing. It is no longer needing to be right.*
—*Anonymous*

When someone tells us a riddle, we may give up
if we don't know the answer. We give up because
we are tired of trying to get it, or because we are
eager to find out what it is.

Giving up in other situations, may be more difficult. We may need to give up eating something
that isn't healthy for us. We may need to give up
trying to win an argument. We may need to give
up old clothes that we love which no longer fit us.
When we don't want to give up, it may be because
we have forgotten the knowledge, health, or peace
of mind we gain by doing so.

In each case, giving up means growth and going
on with our lives. Giving up may mean many different things in different situations, but it does not
mean doing nothing. It means doing what seems
right for us and giving up the expectation that
what happens will be exactly what we want.

*What can I gain by giving up something that is
harmful today?*

*The most beautiful thing we can experi-
ence is the mysterious. It is the source
of all true art and science.*
　　　　　　　—Albert Einstein

　Albert Einstein knew in his heart that the source
of all his knowledge was not himself, but a mys-
tery — something or someone outside himself.
And it left him in awe and wonder. He knew also
that while genius may be ninety percent hard work
and only ten percent inspiration, all the hard work
in the world amounts to nothing without that outside, mysterious inspiration.

　He was right. We can work hard and play hard.
We can paint and draw and write and develop
formulas all our lives, but none of it will be new or
different unless we are open to inspiration from
some power outside ourselves that also, somehow,
is deep within us. To be really good at anything,
whether it's playing baseball, designing fashion
clothing, fixing an engine, or cooking, we must
believe in some creative force that helps us excel.
When we see that force at work, we stand in awe
at the wonderful and mysterious gift we have been
given.

How have I been inspired to discover something?

November 28

for most this amazing day. . .
. . .for everything
which is natural which is infinite
  which is yes.

—e. e. cummings

Let us be thankful today for all simple obvious things: for the sun's rising this morning without our having to awaken it; for another good turn the earth makes today without expecting anything in return; for our ability to know right and wrong by heart. Let us give thanks for all small things that mean the world to us; for bread and cheese and clean running water; for our ability to call our enemies our friends, to forgive even ourselves; for our own bodies, however sagging and worn, which insist on continuing for at least another day.

How much ordinary daily good do I take for granted?

*When written in Chinese, the word cri-sis is composed of two characters —
one represents danger and the other
represents opportunity.*
—John F. Kennedy

Family crises are unavoidable. At times, things
are going to break down. This is no reason to give
up and abandon ship. These breakdowns are the
things which will strengthen our lives together if
we do not lose faith. The Einstein family had a
crisis of sorts when their little boy, Albert, did not
talk until he was four years old. But what looked
like a problem at first did not end up that way in
the long run.

We can expect downhill slides once in a while,
and we may even start to feel full of self-pity. With
faith that these setbacks are meant to help us grow
stronger, we won't waste them and end up having
to face them again and again until we do recognize
their true purpose.

What setback can I use to grow stronger today?

November 30

I've never sung anything that I wasn't ready to sing.

—*Claudia Schmidt*

Most of us are curious about the "olden days" before we were born. We ask our parents what life was like when they were kids, what they did, what they looked like, and what they thought about. But most of us, even those who are parents ourselves, have probably never asked our parents, "Were you ready to go to school, to grow up, to get married, to get a job, to have me?"

So often we are afraid to take even a small new step, afraid of change. We feel so alone in our uncertainty. From our point of view, it often looks as though everybody's ready except us.

Perhaps another way to look at it is that, for most of our lives, readiness really isn't much of an issue. Were we ready to be born? Were we ready to walk, to read, to sing? Maybe we were; maybe not. What's important is what we did, not what we were ready to do. For life is mostly a matter of jumping in feet first shouting, "Here I come, ready or not!"

What am I going to do today, ready or not?

December

December

December 1

Go rich in poverty. Go rich in poetry.
—May Sarton

Poetry lets us put the beauty of nature — the clouds, the flowers, the waterfall — into words. Poetry lets us see that things which appear to be opposites may just be different ways of looking at the same thing. How can we be rich in poverty? Wealth in poverty means finding pleasure in simplicity, finding the core of what's important, and saying it in the fewest possible words.

We are so often caught up in the pursuit of more — more money, more toys, more prestige, that we forget how satisfying the simple things can be. Think of the beauty of a sunset or a walk by the river, the fun of playing in a sandbox or swinging on the swings in the park, or in simply taking time to get something done the right way, without hurry.

What riches lie around me right this moment?

December 2

*When one is a stranger to oneself, then
one is estranged from others, too.*
—Anne Morrow Lindbergh

There's a person inside each of us just itching to be known and loved. But if we don't get to know and love that person, how can we expect anyone else to know us?

That's why it's so important to spend time alone getting acquainted with ourselves. And how do we do that? We can sit quietly with ourselves, thinking and listening. Then we can write our thoughts in a journal, or we can draw or paint them. If we play a musical instrument, we can put our thoughts and feelings into music.

When we make the time and effort to know ourselves, it encourages others to want to know us, too. Since everything we do and feel begins inside us, we must feel good about ourselves in order to feel good about anything else. What wonders we are, that we have all the power we need to make our world a happy one!

How do I feel about myself today?

*I wonder if the snow loves the trees and
fields that it kisses them so gently.*
                    —*Lewis Carroll*

In different times and places, clouds can produce snowflakes, raindrops, or even hailstones.
Each one seems to have its own purpose and mood
as it falls from the sky. The snowflake is the light-
est of these, and so it falls slowly and softly. Rain-
fall can be soft or hard. It sometimes feels angry,
almost cleansing.

No matter how thick the snowfall is, it is still
soft. We can rarely hear it land. It covers the world
in a peaceful white. If we look closely, we can see
that each small snowflake is unique.

Like the snowflakes, each of us has a unique
design. Perhaps what we can learn from the snowflakes is how to gently touch the lives and growing
things around us. Times of anger and rain are necessary, but a soft snowfall brings peace to all
humanity.

How can I show my gentle side today?

December 4

*They were the first. . .self-created peo-
ple in the history of the world. And
their manners were their own business.
And so were their politics. And so, but
ten times so, were their souls.*
            —*Archibald MacLeish*

There once was a child named Yemaya. Even
before she could walk or talk, her mother intro-
duced her to the trees. Yemaya touched them and
they accepted her. They told her she was wonderful and she knew it was true.

As she grew up, Yemaya occasionally met people who said unkind things to her. When this happened, she went back to her trees, who continued
to tell her she was just fine. She couldn't understand what was wrong with those who were mean
to her. Whenever they appeared and insisted on
being mean, she pretended what they said was an
arrow that sailed right by as she stepped out of the
way.

We can do the same. What others say or think is
part of them and their lives, not ours. When we
are wise enough to let go of things that don't belong to us, we will find our own treasures.

What can I step out of the way of today?

My true god is always with me.
I am learning to trust myself. . . .
                                        —Joan Parsons

Sometimes a book we read at a very young age stays with us our whole lives.

One girl loved *Heidi* more than any other book. She always thought about the grandfather's hut. It was a special place in the world — with the fresh mountain air, the spring flowers, the winter fire on the hearth. But the part she carried with her to adulthood was the part about the grandfather pouring goat's milk into a bowl and telling Heidi to drink it all up so she could grow to be healthy and happy.

Now that girl is a woman. Sometimes, when she wants to feel taken care of, she pours herself a bowl of milk. Then she sits down, picks up the bowl with two hands, and drinks out of it like Heidi. She feels comforted and connected to the universe.

The private rituals we discover in childhood can befriend us all our lives, if we let them.

What do I want when I want comfort?

December 6

Believe that life is worth living, and your belief will help create the fact.
—*William James*

Before Orville and Wilbur Wright ever flew the first airplane at Kitty Hawk, they believed flight was possible. They had a picture of it in their minds. The first step in creating anything is to be able to picture it in our minds. If we can picture it as a possibility, we can work to make it happen.

When we were small, we dreamed a thousand dreams about what could happen in our lives. Anything, even magical things, seemed like they could happen, and our world was full of visions. That part of us that believes wonderful, magical things can happen is still in us. It may have been beaten down for a while, but it is still there waiting to help us seek the wonderful, lovely, and good things in life.

Which of my dreams can I work toward today?

*Only people who have joyfully ac-
cepted themselves can take all the risks
and responsibilities of being themselves.*

—*John Powell*

If we have ever gone to school with a black eye,
we know how embarrassing it can be. We feel self-
conscious and ill at ease. Friends come up to us one
after another to ask how we got it. We may want
to stay away from people until the eye is better. All
of us have things about ourselves we have a hard
time accepting. It doesn't have to be as unusual as
a black eye. We may think we're too big, too little,
too slow, not good readers, not good looking
enough, or not popular enough.

We may need to talk about these things with
someone else, so these bits of ourselves we don't
accept won't limit our freedom to grow. By talking
to another, we may find those traits aren't noticed
by anyone but ourselves. We may also find that
what we once thought of as weak points can be
turned to strengths.

What weakness can I turn to a strength today?

December 8

> *If you must love your neighbor as yourself, it is at least as fair to love yourself as your neighbor.*
> —*Nicholas De Chamfort*

We sometimes find it difficult to accept a compliment. We may feel we don't deserve such attention, and point out reasons why the compliment is untrue. When we act this way, we show a lack of love for ourselves.

God teaches us to love our neighbors as ourselves. Yet, before we can love anyone, we must believe we are worthy of the same love. No creature is undeserving of love, God reminds us of that. We can stop hiding behind feelings of unworthiness. There's nothing stopping us but ourselves. Sometimes it takes courage to say thank you when we get a compliment. Let's exercise that courage, and each time we do, we'll find our self-love growing.

When I thank people today, will I have the courage to smile, too?

Faith is the seamstress
who mends our torn belief
who sews the hem of childhood trust
and clips the threads of grief.
        —*Joan Walsh Anglund*

A seamstress takes large pieces of material and cuts them to size. Then, with the help of needle and thread and buttons, she goes to work to create a finished piece. Sometimes, in the beginning, it is hard to imagine a finished product. But the seamstress believes it is possible and goes to work on it.

Faith is like a seamstress. Faith is what can pull all the unfinished pieces of life into some sort of order. Faith is what lets us know we are all right even when life doesn't seem to make sense. We all need the faith to believe our skills and dreams, and even our heartaches can be sewn into a shape that is beautiful and useful.

Our faith is the seamstress who guides the needle, mends the tears, and helps create a shape and meaning to our lives.

How can I show my faith today?

December 10

She must learn to speak
starting with I
starting with We
starting as the infant does
with her own true hunger
and pleasure
and rage.

—Marge Piercy

Once there was a writer who was writing a book for children. He decided to ask his son for ideas. "What would you like to tell other children?" he asked. He thought the boy would say something like "Everybody love everybody." But instead the boy said, "Number one, ignore what your parents say about nutritious food. Number two, don't go to school."

The father laughed and thanked the boy for his ideas, even though they weren't what he expected. He loved his son for being able to feel and express his desires so strongly.

We all have a child within us, no matter how old we are. When we honor that child, we also honor who we have become, and we free ourselves to express our truest feelings.

What does the child within me want to do today?

Feelings are everywhere — gentle.
—J. Masai

Throughout the day we experience many feelings. Losing something makes us angry. Fighting with a friend makes us sad. Perhaps we're lonely because no one is home. Getting an unexpected treat makes us happy. Our feelings come and go just like the hours of our lives.

Letting our feelings be whatever they are is good. They'll go away in time. We may not like all feelings; sadness or anger may be uncomfortable, but being human means we'll have many different feelings each day. If we're quiet with them, they'll help us grow and understand others better, and then they will suddenly be gone, replaced perhaps by a feeling we like more.

Will I be able to accept my feelings today whether I like them or not?

December 12

Patience is needed with everyone, but first of all with ourselves.
—Saint Francis De Sales

One night Sandra was having trouble putting a puzzle together. Angrily, she pushed all the pieces into a huge pile.

"I can't do this," she said. She got up and walked over to the couch and plopped down.

"Let me tell you a story," said her dad, as he sat down next to her. "There was a daughter who helped her dad take care of her baby sister. Again and again, she helped her baby sister stand and try to walk. One day the daughter tried to put a puzzle together but gave up after only a few tries. She had forgotten how many times she had helped her baby sister."

We are all like Sandra, sometimes. We forget to allow ourselves to fail, even though our growth up to now has been a series of failures that we learned from. With patience, we allow ourselves to take chances we might not otherwise explore, and we widen our world of possibilities. Life has been patient with us so far, now it's our turn.

What have I failed at that I can try again today?

To heal ourselves is a reclamation of the power we all have as living beings to live in harmony with the life energy and to fulfill our potential as creatures among many on this planet.
—*Chellis Glendinning*

We live in a world that tells us healing only comes from outside ourselves. To some, it may seem odd to think each of us has the ability to heal ourselves.

How is this possible? Easy — we can do it if we believe we can. Whatever we believe we cannot do will remain beyond our ability. But believing we can heal ourselves gives us access to many healing ways. Self-acceptance is healing. Singing, playing, walking by a river are healing. Even helping others with their problems can be healing to us. There are as many ways of self-healing as there are people in the world. Once we experience what is healing for us, we can go on to discover many more healing acts to share with others.

What healing things do I like to do?

December 14

Each day comes bearing its gifts. Untie the ribbons.
— *Ann Ruth Schabacker*

Today will be filled with surprises, big ones and small ones, like the gifts at a birthday party. Maybe we'll see a friend we haven't seen for a while. Or we'll find something we thought was lost. Whatever happens today will be special, and is meant to help us grow in just the right way.

Growing up doesn't always feel easy. We're expected to be more responsible and thoughtful of others. We're expected to be honest about our feelings and needs. If we're angry or scared, we need to tell someone. Sharing our secret about being afraid relieves us of the fear, and we feel lighter, happier, like after opening a special gift.

When I receive today's gifts, will I stop to appreciate them?

Great symphonies begin with just one note.

—*Priscilla Young Pratt*

Sometimes it's really hard to get going. We put off things we don't want to do, or are afraid to try. We occasionally feel overwhelmed by the size of a job to be done like cleaning out the cellar or reading a long book for a class.

But think a minute. If Beethoven had thought about how complicated it was to write his Ninth Symphony, with all those instruments and voices and notes to blend together, do we really think he would ever have started? But he didn't get overwhelmed. He sat down and wrote just one small note, and then another, and a third. It took him months, but writing one note led to a second, and, one note at a time, he completed it.

We begin the same way with whatever tasks we have ahead of us. Each tiny bit of progress helps us go on to the next part. We begin by reading one page of that book, or taking one box of junk from the cellar. That's all we have to do. The rest will follow almost on its own. The trick is to begin.

What needs to be done today, and how do I start?

December 16

*Because you're not what I would have
you be, I blind myself to who, in truth,
you are.*
— *Madeleine L'Engle*

Sometimes we expect far too much of the people
around us, and because no one can ever live up to
those expectations, we are almost always disappointed. But wouldn't it be better if we just let go,
and let people be who they are? Then we'd be able
to see them as they are — with all their beauty and
goodness in which we take joy, and with all their
faults which we can also see in ourselves.

When we have put someone up on a pedestal,
sculpturing them to fit our needs and desires by
smoothing out the rough edges and creating new
curves here and there, we cannot see the real person underneath our work. All we see is the illusion
we have created. That is denying the person's real
identity and is disrespectful. It's much better for
our friends and for ourselves if we drop our expectations and illusions, and accept them all just the
way they are.

What unfair expectations do I have of others?

Volunteers are the only human beings on the face of the earth who reflect this nation's compassion, unselfish caring, patience, and just plain loving one another.

—*Erma Bombeck*

The most precious time we will ever have we give away by doing volunteer chores to help others get more out of life. There is no material wage for this kind of work, but a host of emotional rewards. The height of volunteer giving is doing an act of kindness or love so quietly that none but ourselves will ever know we had a part in it.

What great humility this can bring to us, who live in a world where selfish people often insist on credit for all their deeds — often things they had nothing to do with.

All we need do is think of all we have received without deserving it or asking for it. By taking part in the giving end of life, we find the true wealth of our own generosity.

What secret gift can I give today?

December 18

*Endurance is nobler than strength, and
patience than beauty.*
        —*John Ruskin*

It's hard to keep from trying to control the lives
of others, especially in a family. We can learn from
the man whose friend drove twenty miles to and
from work on the freeway every day. "How can
you do it?" he asked. "I've tried, and I can't go a
mile in such traffic without screaming at the crazy
drivers who cut in, go too slow, change lanes. Nobody listens. I'd lose my mind if I had to do it your
way." His friend replied, "Your trouble is trying to
drive every car around you. I relax and drive only
one car — my own."

We have only our own lives to live, and this is
usually enough to keep us busy. If we pay too
much attention to how others live, we will neglect
ourselves.

What acts of others can I ignore today?

Open your mind and your heart to be still.

—Shawn Phillips

In this time of international conflict and mistrust it is easy to despair. At times we may even feel hopeless as we hear about wars and weapons. But there is hope! Change can grow from within each of us.

The world is like a tree — if the tree is diseased and the leaves brown and brittle, the gardener does not treat the branches, but tends to the roots. Our world is made up of nations, in which there are states containing communities of neighborhoods where individual people live. *We* are the roots of our world tree. As attitudes change; as we accept and love ourselves honestly and learn, in turn, to accept and love others regardless of our differences, slowly, the branches that extend from us and cover the world will grow strong. The peace we can make within ourselves can be reflected everywhere.

Will I find the peace within myself today?

December 20

Give to the world all that you have,
And the best will come back to you.
— *Mary Ainge De Vere*

When we share something of our own with a friend, it gives both of us a special feeling. Generosity blesses the giver as much as the receiver. Sometimes we feel selfish, wanting to hoard all our treats or treasures. But when we secretly hide them away, we cheat even ourselves from enjoying them.

Giving love and friendship to others works in just the same way. When we express love and kindness to others, we feel more love toward ourselves. Though we may not understand just how it works, we can be certain it does. The more of anything we give away to others, the greater our own rewards will be.

How can I practice generosity today?

*I came to see the damage that was done
and the treasures that prevail.*
— *Adrienne Rich*

It takes great courage to face ourselves — to look honestly and fearlessly at our behavior, especially if we have done and said things we are not proud of. We may have caused a lot of sadness in our own and others' lives. It's not easy to look at.

But let's remember, too, that what we do and say is not all of who we are. And let's also look at the treasures in ourselves — those things we have said and done that have brought great comfort, joy, and love into the lives of others.

Beneath the negative parts of ourselves, deep within us, is a kernel of good. Let's look for that as well, and water it so it can grow — so we can grow into the persons we are meant to be.

What is the best part of me, and how can I share it today?

December 22

> *And the seasons, they go round and*
> *round*
> *And the painted ponies go up and*
> *down*
> *We can't return, we can only look*
> *Behind from where we came*
> *And go round and round and round in*
> *the circle game.*
> — *Joni Mitchell*

High in the mountains near Sun Valley, Idaho, is a small cabin. The cabin is always left open for hikers to rest and refresh themselves. There is food in the cabin and wood for a fire. Often, weary backpackers have arrived there, tired and thirsty, to find just the beverage or snack they needed to help them on their way. The cabin operates on a system of trust — if you use something in the cabin, you replace it with something else. Perhaps it is just the thing the next traveller needs to go on. It is a circle game.

We are all part of a big circle. If we give of ourselves or do a favor for someone, eventually — sometimes years later — someone will do something for us that will help us on our way. We do these little deeds without expecting to be rewarded, and we can accept others' little gifts without feeling forever in someone's debt. These unselfish acts, stored in our mountain cabin, stand ready for the next traveller.

What gift can I pass on to another today?

There are no riches above a sound body, and no joy above the joy of the heart.

—Anonymous

Holidays are a wonderful and exciting time of year — a time to enjoy snowflakes falling, company coming, and presents. Sometimes we find ourselves concentrating soley on the wrapped presents and forgetting about the presents of the heart. With God's help, we can begin to notice such things as the hug from a brother or sister, the laugh of a grandparent or the hand-drawn card given to us by a friend. All of these wonderful presents and more are ours for the taking; we need only to see beyond the wrapped packages. It is then we will fully experience the joys of the heart.

How many gifts do I see around me right now?

December 24

He is Father. Even more, God is Mother, who does not want to harm us.

—Pope John Paul I

God is many things to different people. Some call God "Father," others "Mother," still others "Higher Power," "Inner Light," "Deeper Self," and "Supreme Being."

It doesn't matter what name we use. No one name is ever fully adequate, and each of us has our own private way of trying to understand that which we can't ever understand fully. We give God names which attempt to express what God means to us personally, what God does for us as individuals, and how we see ourselves in relation to God.

Could it also be true that other people can't be labelled and put into one box? Doing so limits them to one particular way of being understood, and it limits the ways we can get to know them. If we are all made in God's image, then we all deserve the freedom to be seen differently by different people.

How does God look to me today?

We have no right to ask, when sorrow comes, Why did this happen to me? unless we ask the same question for every joy that comes our way.
—*Philip S. Bernstein*

All of us have reasons to be grateful. Usually, the word implies we have received something. We often think of gratitude as that warm feeling we get from someone else's generosity. We are particularly grateful when we get unexpected gifts from those who owe us nothing. Within a family, we expect such acts of love because we are close to one another.

But gratitude doesn't always come from being a receiver. Gratitude is warmest when it accompanies the joy of being able to give without expecting anything in return. We find it isn't enough to feel grateful. We have to express our gratitude by showing kindness and service to everyone around us.

Gratitude is the greatest of all heart-openers. When it enters the heart, love pours out. For every kindness we receive, gratitude inspires a hundred acts of giving.

How can I show my gratitude today?

December 26

I take it that what all men are really after is some form of, perhaps only some formula of, peace.
—James Conrad

When snow drifts quietly down on a winter evening, the hush of nature brings a great sense of peace. Each of us has known times like this. Many of these times did not depend on conditions like snow, or soft music. When we are able to keep a quiet center within ourselves, we are truly in tune with the spirit. Peace of the heart comes from a Power greater than ourselves, and from the faith that all of us, and all that happens to us, are part of a great plan.

Just as the snow falls softly, without fear, without regard for whether it will land on a tree bough or in the street, we, too, can live our lives with peaceful acceptance of whatever comes along, knowing it comes to us naturally and from God.

Am I prepared to accept wherever I will land today?

In this sad world of ours, sorrow comes to all, and it often comes with bitter agony. Perfect relief is not possible except with time.

—*Abraham Lincoln*

Time may or may not heal all wounds. It depends on how we use the time. If we deny our sorrow, or run away from it, or hope it will just go away by itself, we will be miserable. But if we turn and face it, and express our sadness in healthy ways, somehow we are transformed by the sorrow itself. While the loss is still there, it begins not to hurt so much.

We can express our sadness in many ways. Crying is probably the healthiest means of expressing grief. It's good to cry, even for men, because it releases tension and stress, and we find a little peace afterwards. It is true that tears are healing.

Getting angry and expressing our anger in appropriate, healthy ways also helps to heal wounds of loss, strange as it may seem. Yes, in time and with the courage to express our feelings, our wounds are indeed healed.

What is a healthy way to express my anger at a loss?

December 28

*I'll walk where my own nature would
be leading —It vexes me to choose another guide. . . .*
                              —Emily Bronte

We journey across many intersections in our
lives. Some may point in two directions, while
others lead off in several. Our choice of direction
can be difficult, especially when our friends
choose a road we know to be dangerous. When
this happens, we can choose to go our own way
without them. If they begin to tease and taunt us
about our decisions, may we remember that they
are as scared as we were about their friends' reac-
tion. We are not, after all, living for someone else.
If we would be leaders, we can be assured that true
leadership comes from following our own directions with confidence that it's right for us, not
from fear of losing others' company.

We can let others live their own lives without us,
if their direction is not for us. We can walk away
with pride, satisfied in the knowledge that we
refused to allow other people's fears change our
decisions.

How have I gone my own way recently?

The price of dishonesty is self-destruction.
                    —*Rita Mae Brown*

There once was a woman who told her husband what she thought he wanted to hear. She told him she was happy when she wasn't. She told him he liked his friends when she didn't. She tried to figure out what he wanted so she could do it for him. She felt hurt when he didn't do the same for her. She felt he should also try to read her mind and do what she wanted without her having to express it. She was scared to tell him how she really felt.

However, her pain and resentment grew so much she couldn't stand it any longer, so she told him her true feelings. He was so used to hearing her lies that he called her a liar when she told the truth. Now she knew how much she had hurt herself by trying to please him at the cost of her own honesty and needs.

Honesty is necessary for a good relationship with anyone. When we lie to ourselves, we cannot tell the truth to others. By being honest, we open our doors to others, we trust them with our true feelings, and they love us for who we really are.

Who can I tell how I really feel today?

December 30

Telling the truth is a pretty hard thing.
— Thomas Wolfe

Lying can be like sailing choppy waters. The more we lie, the higher the waves get, and the harder the sailing. When we lie, we feel we've failed ourselves and others. We have to work hard to cover up our lies, and the fear of someone finding out is always with us.

If we ask God for courage to tell the truth, we can be like the sailboat on a clear and calm day. We can enjoy the small waves and the light warm breeze we've given ourselves. Honesty is a good habit, and is easy. With a little faith in our own worth, we can choose the calm waters' honesty and apply our creativity to new, growth-oriented activities instead of covering up old mistakes.

How can I smooth my waters right now?

Finish each day and be done with it.
Tomorrow is a new day; begin it well.
   —Ralph Waldo Emerson

Two of the most useless phrases in the English language are "what if" and "if only." We waste so much time and energy thinking about what we might have done and wishing we had acted or re-acted differently. We imagine how things might have turned out "if only. . . ."

All of us make mistakes. To go back and wonder and wish about our yesterdays prevents us from living fully today. Each day is a fresh chance; a new beginning. We can only squeeze what we can out of the moment and let the drops fall where they may. Some will evaporate and some will form rainbows.

Can I forget about yesterday and start a fresh new day?

INDEX

Hazelden

Other daily meditation books that may interest you...

Each Day a New Beginning

The first daily meditation guide created by and for women involved in 12 Step recovery programs. Hundreds of thousands of women have found help in this collection of thoughts and reflections that offers hope, strength, and guidance every day of the year. Our number two bestseller. (400 pp.)
Order No. 1076A

Twenty-Four Hours a Day

The original daily meditation book. Our all time bestselling book, *Twenty-Four Hours a Day* was first published in 1954. Since then, over 3 million people throughout the world have used this classic "little black book" to guide their recovery one step at a time, one day at a time. (384 pp.)

Thank you for the book Twenty-Four Hours a Day. *My copy is now 14 years old, but I assure you the message is as crisp and applicable as the first day I picked it up. Truly an inspirational work!*

--Elmer S.

Order No. 1050A